MY DEEPEST HEART'S DEVOTIONS 2

AN AFRICAN WOMAN'S DIARY - BOOK 2

GERTRUDE KABATALEMWA

Edited by NONA BABICH AND TERESA SKINNER
Photography by ALISA ALBERS
Photography by TERESA SKINNER

ISBN: 978-1-950123-21-6

Copyright © 2019 by Teresa Skinner

Unless otherwise indicated, all Scripture quotations are taken from the Holy Bible, King James Version - Public Domain Scripture quotations marked (ESV) ® Bible (The Holy Bible, English Standard Version®), copyright © 2001 by Crossway, a publishing ministry of Good News Publishers. Used by permission. All rights reserved."

Scripture quotations marked (NIV) are taken from the Holy Bible, New International Version®, NIV®. Copyright © 1973, 1978, 1984, 2011 by Biblica, Inc.™ Used by permission of Zondervan. All rights reserved worldwide. www.zondervan.com The "NIV" and "New International Version" are trademarks registered in the United States Patent and Trademark Office by Biblica, Inc.™

All rights reserved.

No part of this book may be reproduced in any form or by any electronic or mechanical means, including information storage and retrieval systems, without written permission from the publisher, except for the use of brief quotations in a book review.

*Gone so soon,
with all the dedicated work she had done...
we will continue with the work she has left behind.
showing people "God's Love and Care"
Emmanuel Mwesigye*

On left - Gertrude Kabatalemwa as a young girl

CONTENTS

Foreword	xi
1. Do Not Look for Easy Come and Ready Made Life	1
2. Love of God is Not Automatic	5
3. The Chicken Message	7
4. After Obedience There Is Always A Reward	9
5. Storms	13
6. He is Closer Than Your Heart	17
7. Do Not Look at People, Look at Me	23
8. Six Cages	25
9. The Sovereignty of God Overshadows Our Incompetencies	29
10. Ambush Fasting	31
11. Ask What You Want	37
12. Be Yourself, Be Natural	45
13. Called of the Lord to be Prepared	51
14. The Lord is Faithful, He Will Make You Strong	57
15. Waiting for His Bride	61
16. The Lord Does Not Stand Rebellion	65
17. Akangonza Yesu Akangonza	71
18. Consider Your Ways!	75
19. The Grace and Smile of My God	81
20. I Have Your Name in My Secret Heart	85
21. A Dance of Jesus	91
22. Chulera Webundaze	97
23. Prayer for Tooro Kingdom	101
24. Be Faithful to be Filled, Ba Mwesigwa	107
25. I am plan B	113
26. Wisdom Spoke	121
27. Genuine Doors and a False Door	127
28. Do Not Choose Doors by Their Appearance	133

29. Deception of the Enemy	137
30. No Man Is Worthy to Succeed Until He Is Willing to Fail	143
31. Hope, What is Hope?	145
32. How to Overcome Fear	147
33. I Am Standing for My Nation Uganda	151
34. Prosperity Gospel	155
35. The Deep Dark Forest	157
About the Author	161

WORD OF THE LORD FOR GERTRUDE KABATALEMWA

*I believe I heard the Lord say
You are a General - in His army
You are a woman of valor
You are a woman of great faith
Those who have preceded you and those that will follow*

*There is not one with a greater faith as you
You are an Apostle - there will be more churches established
Training up those in your care now to begin other church groups
As His message of salvation and love continues to be spread
throughout the nation*

*I believe I heard the Lord say
Your job is not done
You have accomplished much but
There is much more to be accomplished
He has given you a great vision
And those to stand with you in bringing forth this vision
You cannot do this alone*

I believe I heard Him say

Begin to seek Him
There are those who are now working in various projects
But He will begin to show you - one by one-
Those whom He will raise up to walk beside you
To further along and to fulfill the vision
Walking with you in unity, harmony and one accord
To accomplish the same vision He has given you
You to delegate responsibility for various projects to those He shows you
So that you can be freed up to begin new endeavors
And to further along others

Multiplication - multiplication of help - more people to be set in place to help you
To take on more of the work that needs to be done
Delegation - your delegating more work to others to free up yourself

He will continue to provide for you
Finances help in all you need
The vision is expanding
More will be started
More will be accomplished

And I believe I hear the Lord say
The angels of the Lord encamp around you
And continue to be at your side
To protect you and provide for the needs
Rest in peace knowing that even greater things are in store
Greater things will be accomplished

And I believe I hear the Lord say
You have been found faithful

He loves you very much

And the Lord says to you
"Well done My good and faithful servant!"

Sunday Mar 28, 2010 Approximately 5:20 PM

FOREWORD

We may not agree with what Ms. Gertrude Kabatalemwa has written. It may not be politically correct for our generation. But, let us get passed our judgements, and hear the heart of this African woman.

If so, we will find ourselves understanding a depth of spirituality that will most likely be lost to the next generations.

AFRICA HAS SOMETHING TO SAY TO US.

May we listen intently with raw ears to hear a direction that could keep our future from becoming sterile.

Teresa Skinner
All Nations International

CHAPTER ONE

DO NOT LOOK FOR EASY COME AND READY MADE LIFE

DO NOT LOOK for Easy Come and Already Made Life, and learn to work for yourself. For even when we were with you, we used to give you this order; if anyone is not willing to work, then he is not to eat, either. For we hear that some among you are leading an undisciplined life doing no work at all, but acting like busy bodies, 2 Thes. 3:10-11. Brethren, train yourselves to work for your needs and do not be taken with easy come, you will find yourself in the situation which you will not solve yourself or which may end you in death. Easy come. Easy Go. Easy come, easy go comes with conditions like if you want to get rich bring me your most beloved child for a sacrifice, so that you will get all the money you want.

Craving for already made life. Do not look for already made things, always they have strings attached, they are baits, the enemy uses and catches his prey. Look at the one who s giving you a gift ask yourself why in the long run he/she will ask you to pay back? And when the time of paying back comes he may ask you to do the impossible. Illustration of a saved lady who worked in Kikuubo, how she wanted also to make quick sales and ended under water. Also, a man who wanted to Succeed in his ministry using worldly tricks and he ended in a crocodile's belly.

Pastors who seek after missions, Pastors be careful with easy come and do not seek after them, fix your eyes on Him who called you, He is able to supply all your needs according to His riches in Glory, Philippians 4:19. Do not seek after outside missions or donors who are giving free money. I know a pastor who went to the US seeking for who to give him easy breakthrough, he ended in an occultic church. When he returned, he was no longer preaching Christ but what the occultic agents told him to say, he became a "Jesus Only" agent.

Lazy-body, the devil will give you what to do. If you are lazy and you do not want to work for yourself the devil will give you means of how you can earn easy life, by just sitting, you will be a queen, worshiped, honoured, driven by chauffeurs who opens and shuts the door for you.

I had a close relative who used to hold herself as a queen, and wanted all the easy life, she would say, "I do not want my life to be harassed with the hassles of this world." When she was young, as soon as she completed her University, she married a high-ranking officer who later was made an Ambassador and they lived abroad. That life was really befitting the young beautiful lady; but later she separated with her husband, the ambassador, and immediately caught up with another man who was supposed to be a cultural king, and she was having a good job in a high office where she was a protocol officer, just to meet diplomats, meet visiting foreign dignitaries, and travel.

As she wanted easy life, being a queen was her goal, but as I told you, easy life comes with hard conditions. In 2008, the cultural king had another traditional wife who was not educated. So, he wanted to make my relative an official wife. The first condition he gave her was to resign her high job in order to marry him.

You know the devil is a liar, first he blinds you and makes you deaf so that you cannot hear, he will not allow you to see beyond your nose, even if somebody tells you "there is a pity, do not go beyond," you will not listen.

This lady blindly went ahead and resigned her prestigious job to go and become an official wife, which was a lie of the devil. Soon after resigning her job, this would be king got so sick and was hospitalized. When she went to visit him already his concerned subjects were surrounding his bed. When they mentioned her arrival, the only word she got was "She Is A Murderer who wanted to kill our king! He does not want even to see you at all at all."

If you want Already Made Life, you could end by losing everything. My friend be careful if you want Already Made Life, you may end up by losing even whatever little you have put in your effort. The devil is not kind at all, the above lady lost her job on condition that she is going to become an official wife, a queen, she lost her job, never got what was promised her to be official wife, a queen.

Spend time working out something, however little, but faithfully, dedicatedly done, when the Lord comes and asks you what do you have in your hands that I can bless you with? e.g. a Zerephath widow, with her little handful flour and oil which she prepared bread for a man of God, Elijah, 1 Kings 17:8-16 and 2 Kings 4:1-7.

Do not look for Already Made Life young lady, you may want to hunt for an easy game and find a charged buffalo. You may want to get men who have already made their money and are married, and you sister, you say I do not care this is a share world even if I am the fifth. A lady in Ntinda, young as she was, went knowing the man was married, he worked his riches with his old wife but this one wanted already made life which was easy for her. The old wife went and hired gunmen, as the young lady was fully pregnant, she was basking in the early morning sun with her toddler, the gunman showered her with bullets she died, her toddler and the unborn. Wanting ready made life can be risk taking and costly.

Ask God to show you, your own mine, where you are going work and feel contented and be fulfilled and give God the Glory.

8th October 2009

CHAPTER TWO

LOVE OF GOD IS NOT AUTOMATIC

JESUS IS THE WORD, John 1:1-3 and 14

His name was called the word of God, Revelations 19:13

God asks Moses to gather His people together and learn to fear God, Deut. 4:29

Thy word have I his in my heart, that I might not sin against thee, it is a lamp to my feet, Psalm 119:11, 105

LOVE OF GOD IS NOT AUTOMATIC, IT GROWS THRU SEEKING, SEARCHING, AND SETTING STRATEGIES.

The Lord spoke to me that: "The Word and Love of God is not Automatic, it grows thru seeking, searching, and setting strategies. The Holy Spirit said; the Word or Love of God is built like a brick wall, here you build brick by brick, one at a time. That if you expect to get automatic love it will be meaningless, there has to be an added value. If you get it automatically you will not handle it with care. It has to be earned in order to gain value for it."

After some time the Holy Spirit guided me to the kitchen and said put a cup in the sink, open the tap and close it until it starts to release just a drop at a time; now go back to your bedroom. I did as was instructed. After some time, the HS said go back to the kitchen now. When I returned the cup was full. And He said; That is how the Word or Love of God works, one drop at a time, towards the end until one is filled up. He said some people take a long fast seeking the love of God or to know the Word of God. At times they make their body suffer for nothing, at times when they are in the process the enemy intercepts their fast.

You should not alert the enemy that on such and such a day you are going to fast, for reasons known to you. That we should exercise Ambush Fasting, when you have not given warning. And that you can also exercise Drip Fasting you jump to one particular favourite thing you like to eat, drink, do or enjoy and give it up for a particular time when the enemy is unaware. Another time you do another fast without repeating the same thing. That Drip Fasting does not task you but you really feel it, i.e. you go for dinner immediately they bring a good chicken or a dish you enjoy very much, as you start salivating for it. Surrender and say for the sake of the situation I am going through I will fast this, you continue like that where the enemy will not guess what your next move is.

CHAPTER THREE

THE CHICKEN MESSAGE

TOWARDS THE END of the year around 29th December 2009, I was in the village again talking fasts on the same topic.

The Holy Spirit said to me, "Give me the comparison of an Organic Chicken and a Broiler Chicken.

- Natural – Artificial
- Brings own chicks – Comes out of Hatchery
- Looks after its chicks – Does not have chicks
- Grows with time – Forced growth
- Warns its chicks of danger – Does not mother instinct
- Helps people to tell time – Does not know about time
- Warns people when there is danger – Does not know to warn of danger
- Strong body and bones – Weak body and bones
- Runs fast if there is danger – Does not know how to run
- Fights its enemies – Easily picked for food
- Good flavor – No flavor
- Looks for own food and water – Fed food & water

- Basks in natural light – Basks in man made light
- Looks at the sun – Does not look at the sun

The Holy Spirit asked me that "When you prepare these chickens do they give you that same aroma or taste?" This is because two chickens are different, so are the two Christians in a Church, the one who scratches for self is naturally grown and the one who waits to be fed is a broiler and does not grow strong and develop muscles. They cannot run or Fight in times of danger, and is easily picked for food because he does not know the truth or the lie because he does not scratch for word for himself. But the natural Christian has all the values for she seeks, searches, scratches, waits upon the Lord has the natural wisdom. 9th September 2009

CHAPTER FOUR

AFTER OBEDIENCE THERE IS ALWAYS A REWARD

AND HE SAW two boats lying at the edge of the lake, but the fishermen had gotten out of them and were washing their nets. He got into one of the boats, which was Simon's and asked him to put out a little way from the land. He sat down and began teaching the people from the boat, Luke 5:2. Jesus did not have a Public Address System, when we talk of away from the land it must have been about hundred meters which is a bit far for one's voice to cover the multitude, as Jesus used to draw big crowds. This was divine power.

When He had finished speaking, He said to Simon, Put out into the deep water and let down your nets for a catch, Luke 5. Peter had spent the whole night toiling and caught nothing and by the time Jesus found them they were washing their nets. Jesus is a rewarder, He cannot use your property and not pay you back and when He pays. He triples, quadruplicates, even a hundred folds. After using Simon's boat Jesus knew because He is God that Simon and group had worked hard throughout the night and caught nothing. Jesus rewarded him with a big catch of fish, because He had used his boat.

Simon, though he knew that throughout the night they caught nothing, said "I will do as you say and let down the nets." Obedience. We need to obey when God says something because whenever He says something, He knows the reason why. He asked me in 1980s "Why do you waste much time Plaiting hair for so many hours?" I used to sit for 8 hours on the knees of those dirt Nubian women, on a sewage, because I wanted to seek for outside beauty.

Again in 1998 as I was pencil lining my eye brows, the Lord spoke to me in an audible voice said "Do you think that pencil adds any beauty on you, why do not you seek the inner beauty?" I looked at the pencil and swore to the Lord that from that day I will never use that eye pencil liner, and started to depend on the inner beauty which is given by the creator.

After obedience there is always a reward, When they had done this, they enclosed a great quantity of fish, and their nets began to break, so they signaled to their partners in the other boat for them to come and help them, Luke 5:6. The reward was so big. Jesus is God, He knew this when He told Simon to let down the nets. As He was preaching all the fish came to listen to the sermon of the King of kings; as He was preaching all the creation was listening to Him even the water was still, because the boat was not being carried by the waves it had to obey its Creator.

So, even you when you are doing the right thing and right with God all eternity is behind you, the creation will Listen and obey. When the Lord wanted to destroy the earth with the flood and He asked Noah, the righteous man, to make a boat and collect all creatures two by two. Guess what order did he issue to bring all the creatures in pairs from different environments, deserts, forests, savannah, tropical, ocean, tundra. When Moses lifted the rod the Red Sea parted. When Joshua was Fighting he commanded the sun and the moon to stand until he finished with his enemies, Joshua 10:12-14.

But when Simon Peter saw that, he fell down at Jesus' feet saying "Go away from me Lord, for I am a sinful man," Luke 5:8. Repentance. Simon Peter repented before Jesus when he realized his spiritual state. You also need to know your spiritual state. Many people have gone on and on thinking when they got saved things were ok, yet they fell from the grace long time ago. When one is drifting, he does not understand, one falls when is still standing, 2 Chronicles 16:1-14.

After acknowledging your spiritual state, Jesus said to Simon "Do not fear, from now on you will be catching men," Luke 5:10. The call on Peter: Until you repent, that is when the Call comes through. God cannot use people who have not made it right with Him. He uses people who have recognized the spiritual state of affairs of their soul. After that Simon Peter, James and John left everything and followed Him. After repenting when the call comes, you do not hold on to anything, except to follow wherever he leads you. Some people do not want to leave everything and follow Him for fear of some petty, petty nick-nacks. They say now if I completely leave everything and follow, what about selling my liquor, what about the man or boy, whom I am still hoping is going to marry me, or has been looking after me. 16th October 2009

Children who lived in the village house

CHAPTER FIVE

STORMS

MESSAGE. Grace, Ephesians 2:8-9.

My heart was so down and so much grieved. The previous week was so bad for me after reading Bukedde Newspaper where a former student, was displayed with a man who stole 500m/= from her. I was condemning and judging her, how she could do such a thing. As we were going back home, I stopped to buy some provisions at the road side stall. I bought tomatoes worth 2000/=, onions worth 3,000/=, greens worth 1,000/=, but the tomatoes were more than a kilo I paid the man 6,000/=. He came after me that I had taken 2 kilos of tomatoes and I gave him more 1,000/= and I walked away. But there was a witness inside me that I did wrong and started feeling guilty for stealing the tomatoes.

The Spirit witnessed in my heart that "It is by His grace otherwise no one can boast of being good at all on his own, that any one is liable to do anything if it is not the Grace of God." 24th October 2009

The Storm, after dismissing the crowd Jesus asked His disciples to get in the Boat and He went to sleep because he was tired. The storm, wind and rain came down and the boat was filling fast and the disciples started scooping water until no more, until they remembered that Jesus was in the boat sleeping and they went to wake Him up. When He woke up He calmed the storm and the disciples were amazed. Luke 8:22-25.

Jesus could not just go to sleep soundly like that. Everybody has a storm of: Family, sickness, enemies, children, parents, debts, barren women, widowhood, orphaned, loosing parents or children. You need to Wake Up Jesus and He will calm the storm. Some people are in the storm and Jesus is Sleeping and they do not know how to wake Him up. At times Jesus is so kind when He sees you are having a storm, He will go and ask one of the believers who know that Jesus is in the boat sleeping and the believer will wake Him up for you.

Example, on 19th November 2009 I knew a gentleman who was in a storm and his boat was in danger, Jesus took me to his home and showed me what was happening and told me to pray for him. I went to the village with a couple to ministers to minister. I returned to Kampala, the Lord again showed me a deep wound which was in the gentleman's head and his arms which were turning like an albino. I asked the Lord how I was going to meet that person and pray for him because he is not a believer and he protests very much of Born-Again Beliefs. I made a decision that I was going to take a three day fast, 12 hours a day. In the Evening the Lord brought him back to me in a dream that I was at home, I saw him coming and kneeling down for prayers and I laid hands on him for his cure.

You need to wake up Jesus and He will calm the storm. Another example of one boy who had taken poison when He asked me to pray for him. Our Lord cares, if you do not know how to wake Him up, He will tell someone to wake Him up for you.

Some storms are Regions, National or District levels. Wars, famine, disease, rebel's activities, inversions, calamities like earthquakes, floods, hurricanes, and even Godlessness. Still the Lord wants His praying people to wake Him up, and if a nation does not have its people praying, He will ask people of other nations who know how to wake Him up depending on the trust and obedience of the one who is asked to pray. The Lord makes a choice of whom to wake Him up, e.g. in 1984 four American Journalists were hostages in Palestine and going to be executed by Palestine terrorists, then in 1989 there was the bloody coup of Philippines.

Our Lord cares, He sent Peter to the house Peter the Tuner to go to Cornelius's house because Cornelius used to do good. When the storm came to his board, the Lord remembered to send Peter to go and wake Jesus to calm the storm. Dorcas, when she was dead the house was full people wailing and showing all the good hand works she had done to the people, Acts 9:36-40. The Lord caused Peter to go and Wake Him to calm the storm and raise Dorcas from the dead.

Your boat is rocking back and forth by the storms of this World, you do not know that Jesus is at the back sleeping and needs to be awakened or you are not doing anything good which can cause the Lord to send you His obedient servant to come and wake Him for you. Therefore, brother, sister do something which will cause the Lord to send you His servant when there is a storm in your boat or always be aware that Jesus is sleeping at the back of your boat, whenever there is a storm just walk to the back of the boat and wake Him up and He will come and calm the Storm. 5th - 7th December 2009

CHAPTER SIX

HE IS CLOSER THAN YOUR HEART

KASOZI PRAYER MOUNTAIN,

Theme: Why are people handcuffing themselves when Jesus has set them free?

Because of Lack of Knowledge, people have joined salvation as a club, society, worldly grouping. Women have joined others as a matter of rivalry. Men have joined to look for women and women to look for men. Handcuffed for Excitement of joining for music and entertainment. Competition in joining that so and so is saved, I will also get saved. Problems, so people have got saved to solve their problems that are handcuffs.

Because of Lack of Faith, People, do not look and Depend on People, but to Him. Cheating is corruption and is a self handcuff. Keeping a deaf ear to the Voice of God handcuffs many. Wrong Motives as doing something for wrong end results. Lack of Transparency as one comes secretive. Because of the Lack of the Word and not studying the word keeps one under bondage. Because of Familiar Spirits and Familiarizing Spirits. Pride handcuffs when we say "I know I have heard all that, I have been in salvation for 10, 20 years." People no longer have the fear of the Lord, Luke

1:50, Psalm 103:17. People are changing the Word to fit their egos, (Yesu ye Mwami wange). Mixing Godly songs to fit worldly ones for gains, for publicity, etc. Calling God human titles, e.g. The Old Man, Muzei, or Boyfriend handcuffs growth of our freedom.

Prayer, Lord, help Loose those handcuffs and let us Trust, trust Jesus in all; your family, business, health, etc. Lead us to Meditate on His Word day and Night. Show us how to give Him 100%. Your Word Lord is hidden in my heart so that I may not sin against you, Psalm 119:11. Your Word is settled in heaven, Psalm 119:89. Everything has its limits and end, i.e. fame, riches, academic, etc. Psalm 119:96. Restrain our feet, eyes, ears to hear. Receive, love and obey the Word; Psalm 119:101. Your Word is a Lamp unto my feet and a light into my path, Psalm 119:105. Amen. 30th December 2009

BEFORE I WENT TO SLEEP AT 1.00AM I WAS DISTURBED because I wanted to know where the scripture is saying when you will separate the evil from the good then I will make your mouth my mouth piece. I determined to try and look for it, or at least read the Word of God. As I opened the Bible straight away my right thumb was on Jeremiah 15:19.

Early in the morning in the spirit I saw myself making holes in the bones, longish like porcupine quills and passing thread through them presenting a Word of God. Then I saw this thread coming from the head and going through every bone in the skeleton of a man, and the thread remaining on the head attached to the Spirit of God. He created eternity in the heart and no man can ..., Ecclesiastes 3:11. I imagined that thread was like light, lighting the whole inside and outside. The thread was lighting the marrows, veins, muscles; no diseases inside and out could lodge anywhere without the thread-light revealing it.

The Lord asked me a secret question and I answered: Lord your Word is everything I need the Only Request I made for 2010: to overflow with the Word from Genesis to Revelation. That as the enemy tries to come, he will find the Word like a Fountain with a cleansing flows with me standing in the middle.

Your Word Lord, I know it is You, Yourself, John 1:1.

> It is Wisdom.
> It is Power.
> It is Treasure.
> It is Authority.
> It is Understanding.
> It is Knowledge.
> It is Healing.
> It is Beauty.
> It is All in All.
> It is life Provider.
> It is Love.
> It is Joy.

Your Word, O!!! Lord, is hidden in my heart that I may not sin against you, Psalm 119:11.

Lord your Word is a lamp unto my feet and a light unto my path, Psalm 119:105. 13th January 2010

GOD NEXT TO YOUR HEART, AFTER PRAYERS EARLY IN THE

morning the Lord spoke to me, "Many people do not know how close God is to us." That He is closer than your heart!!! Whatever you are doing the Lord is next to your heart seeing and hearing you. Your Word, Lord, I have hidden in my heart that I may not sin against you, Psalm 119:105.

In the evening I was in the presence of God of Love till late in the morning of 26th, I was swimming in the River of His Presence as per His message above. I declared that being in this experience and You walking with me to Heaven like Enoch is my pleasure and leave me here till You come back, still it is my desire to tell all nations, languages and colours of all continents about your saving power.

I said, Lord, at times I feel that I haven't fasted, seeked or waited upon You Lord enough for You to use me. Witness inside me said "that is where many people are going wrong." You may do all that, but do them with wrong motive and get a familiarization, fake anointing, e.g. a lady who used to fast for Power to do miracles and see constant miracles, but she got a wrong anointing which resulted in a cult of church.

We should fast, seek and wait upon the Lord with care and humility as the Spirit of the Lord leads, but not to force yourself into it as if to twist the hand of the Lord to force Him to give you what you want. He told me many people have their calling. God gave them their Ministry but many have run away from their calling and joined ministries where they were not called, i.e. if God called to you to sing and to bring 10,000 souls, and for you, you saw that being a Pastor suits you better than singing, you are being disobedient. There is no reward for you in Pastoring ministry where you were not called. When you meet the Lord he will ask you, I called you to be good Musician and you sent yourself to Pastorship. You were supposed to bring in 10,000 souls and they are all lost because of your disobedience, because each call has its anointing. People are entering in ministries which are not theirs.

I grew in a village going through all the chores with goats, cows, gardening, fetching.

Water, catching grasshoppers, hunting butterflies, you name it. Every time the Lord talks to me he talks to me on those lines. On this issue He showed me harvesting in a garden of millet, our mum used to give each one a piece rate in the area they perform best thus one in harvesting millet, one to dry up peanuts, another to guard millet against birds, yet another one to remain home preparing food for the workforce. Therefore, each one was to do his/her best to perform her/his duty well. One could not go jump to do a task which he has not been assigned and each one was to be rewarded according to how he/she has done her task.

However, this is what is happening now in the ministry, people are jumping from one ministry to another where they were not assigned. If the supervisor happens to come and find you in a Ministry where He did not call you. You will not get the Reward. 25th - 26th January 2010

Daughter, Clare Businge with Gertrude Kabatalemwa

CHAPTER SEVEN

DO NOT LOOK AT PEOPLE, LOOK AT ME

SINCE I STARTED to make arrangements to go to the USA my heart was still not excited as usual when I am going to travel. On this day when I returned from the village after meeting someone to assist me with the sponsoring of children I remembered the Word the Lord gave me in 2005 when I was so perturbed by my haste to return to Uganda after Sis Judi told me that a pastor was coming to Uganda with with this brother to assist me, but to my surprise it was a visa versa. My heart was so disturbed until the Lord said "Do not look at people, Look at me."

Prayer, Lord, let nothing in this World excite me, even if they tell me am going to be a President of the whole world or I am given million, billion or trillion dollars on my account. But let me always be excited or moved by the Work the Lord is doing in my spiritual life, by men and women who Fight evil for the sake of righteousness and I will be excited by Soul Winning for the Lord. Lord, give me a Universal smile and countenance, give me spiritual eyes which can penetrate in the sun where no one can see, see underworld through the rocks, through the water at the bottom of the sea, and thru people and say only what you tell me to say. Let my eyes be your window.

Prayer, Lord, let nothing in this world scares me even if it is a New Clear War Head power, an earthquake like the one which hit Haiti, 9/11 crash of planes in the Twin Towers, even the charge of a lion towards me I will not run, I will not hide, I will stand and call on the name of the Lord the creator of Heaven and Earth. In this world let me be scared of my life only When I realize that I have sinned before the Lord, as Disobedience is Sin. I pray let this prayer be heard in the Courts of your Presence and grant me whatever I have petitioned you Lord. Amen. 2nd *February* 2010

OF COURSE, THE LORD USUALLY CALLS YOU TO DO THAT which you are not trained to do! He doesn't call the equipped. He equips the called. He prepares those He has called and He doesn't always call those who are Prepared.

Rees Howells is the intercessor from Wales whom God, the Holy Ghost had trained to defeat Hitler during WWII by prayer. The Lord always made him stand in absolute faith, without wavering, without one penny for the property. He wanted him to acquire the works He wanted him to do, he began, an orphanage, a school and residence for missionaries' children and founded the Bible College of Wales, all of which were accomplished by faith. 11th *May* 2010

CHAPTER EIGHT

SIX CAGES

THE HOLY SPIRIT is not predictable, tamed or tracked as the word says that you cannot tell where the wind blows so is the Holy Spirit's Movement. This makes Christian Life a grand adventure when it chases trackless, matchless Holy Spirit. At opportunity cost you seize the opportunity to follow adventurous Holy Spirit in order to minister to those who are stuck in ignorance, poverty, pain and spiritual slumber and to hear about the love of God.

Six cages that keep us from flowing freely with the Holy Spirit and living the spiritual adventure God destined us.

The cage of responsibility, Many people have considered their responsibilities more than the call God has called them to do, and responsibility stood in the way and blocked the calling.

The cage of routine, The routine cage has become a trap to many people as the say goes "As it was in the beginning is now and ever shall be" our God is a God of variety, He made different colours, languages, creatures, vegetation, seasons, etc. Why do you repeat a prayer from the time you were born? You found it there, and it is still ther. Why do you not disrupt that routine or change it to fit your situation?

The cage of assumptions, Our Assumptions keep us from following the Holy Spirit, one claims "I am too old to get into that, I am young I have still time to have fun, I am educated and well known how will people see me joining such groups, I am not educated I cannot communicate effectively, its soon or its too late to get into that venture."

The cage of guilt, Many people have missed it because they keep blaming and condemning themselves. Some they keep bringing up the past, if I stand to give testimony people still remember what I did or lived, that will keeps you undercover in steady of witnessing for the Lord. So, what if they remember God remembers no more. The enemy keeps you in remembrance of your past, then you remind him of his Future and let him not keep you under. As long as you are focused on what you've done wrong in the past, you won't have energy left to have kingdom dreams.

The cage of failure, Divine detours and divine delays are the ways God get us where He wants us to go. You should always remember that at times your plans are delayed to come to pass due to the fact that God is Networking to fit situations together in favour of you. He may stop your plan when He knows where you are going to construct your building because in the future there is going to be a flood in that area and who ever built there will have to abandon the place. He may let the girl you want to marry disappoint you and marry another man, where as He has saved you from AIDS which could not be identified at first stage (Bill's story).

The cage of fear, The Lord gives us the spirit of love, joy, peace and a sound mind but not the spirit of fear. We need to quit living as if the purpose of life is to arrive safely at death and go to heaven. Instead we need to start playing offense with our lives. The world needs more daring people with daring plans, to put the devil on the run. We need to let the devil warn his demons that if you are going to Gkk, - go at your own risk, your blood is on own head. 12th May 2010

REV. AGNES I NUMER AND GERTRUDE KABATALEMWA

CHAPTER NINE

THE SOVEREIGNTY OF GOD OVERSHADOWS OUR INCOMPETENCIES

I LEFT for LA for the funeral of Sis Agnes Numer; we left Entebbe at 10.00am and arrived London at 5.40 pm.

27th July 2010

MESSAGE AT JFK AIRPORT NEW YORK: WHEN THE Sovereignty of God overshadows our Competencies (Obusobozi/Enkora ya Ruhanga kuswekerra obutesobora bwaitu).

1. Sarah's 90 years of age could not allow her to have or bear a child.
2. Joseph's Status could not open a door for him to be a Prime Minister of Egypt.
3. David's ability took only one stone killing a Giant, or a shepherd boy's job description fits an administrator as king and ruler.
4. Mordecai, a gate keeper, taking on the job of Haman as the Prime Minister.

5. Samson's strength, when the sovereignty power overshadowed him, 300 foxes presented themselves in pairs and he sent them with fire in the fields of the Philistines. When he shouted the Spirit of the Lord came on him mightily and the ropes which bound him broke up, he picked a jaw of a donkey and killed 1000 men.
6. Mary, the mother of our Lord, a virgin knew her incompetency to conceive when she was a virgin, but the angel declared that "The Holy Spirit will come over you and the Power of the Most High will Over Shadow you.

When the sovereignty of God overshadows our incompetencies the results can only be attributed to one thing "The Favour of God" where God does something for us that we could never do ourselves.

28th July 2010

Gertrude Kabatalemwa 1967

CHAPTER TEN

AMBUSH FASTING

STARTED AMBUSH FASTING.

Word of Knowledge, The Market of Kisekka had burnt the previous day. As I was praying the Word of knowledge came to me: Everyday people wake up, something has happened and wonder whether they are dreaming and it will be over, yet it is a reality. A beloved one has died, a child, mum, dad or a friend. Some wake up wishing that another day would not come, because the next day is a day of burial, divorce, judgment, or persecution. Or it could be the excitement of a big promotion, marriage, engagement, introduction party, travel, a baby is born, a business venture, a trophy in sports or graduation. One would wish for the day not to end as long as the excitement lasts.

To those who know the Lord, it is another day the Lord has made "We will rejoice and be glad in it," Psalm 118:24. You wake up expectantly that the Lord is going to do another good thing in your life. You wake up singing a new song every morning it is like a Christmas day.

What is your wakeup call like? Without Christ in the Center of your life there will be upheavals, regrets, disappointments, hurts, and pain but with Christ in the Center of your life it is calm as on the sea of Galilee after the storm. *1st September 2010*

I WOKE UP WITH QUESTIONS FOR MYSELF: (Q) What excites you most? (A) What excites me most is to think that Jesus Christ is returning on the Earth soon. That every day, I am living is drawing me closer to that day.

(Q) What hurts you most? (A) What hurts me most is to see many people are going to go to hell, yet the truth has been given to them and many Christians are doing nothing!!! *2nd September 2010*

MESSAGE, I STARTED BY RECALLING WHEN I WENT BACK TO the village and started women and school projects, people said that I wanted to join politics and was looking for votes. I denied it because politics have never been my goal and I have never considered politics as a good project to invest in, basing on the over view of corruption in the country and the world at large. The Holy Spirit spoke to my heart that to enter politics you have to set Campaign stands to win people's way of understanding by lying, promising people air, abusing, mudslinging, Fighting, accusing of opponents and at times getting embarrassed yourself, E.g.

I remember one Ambassador stood in elections in his area. When he was young he stole a pig, as he stood on a pavilion one man shouted asking him about the pig he stole when they were still in the village. Another man from Tooro who was a Vice President of Obote was during Campaigns people came with rotten eggs and threw them at him in the face, what an Embarrassment.

The Holy Spirit said "The Lord sets Campaign stands for His chosen people without them participating. He plays behind scene and creates Campaign stands for them where no one can stand out with an embarrassing question or throw rotten eggs. He brings them out of 'Unbelievable' scenes and scenarios then places them on a pinnacle where everyone is dumb founded."

Joseph, Prime Minister in Egypt.

A dreamer, he had dreams and shared with his family and some members of his family were biased and when a chance presented itself, they sold him to slavery saying "let us see what will happen to his dreams."

A slave, he was taken as a slave to Egypt, which brought him closer to his dreams which his brothers wanted to kill.

Training, the Lord placed him in the house of Potiphar to be trained in palace protocol.

Persecuted, after training he was to leave the comfort of Potiphar's home and go to the next call to prepared for the task ahead;

Prison, the next level of preparation was in prison. The Lord sent him two palace officials to bring him a gate pass to the palace. They presented him their dreams.

Interpreter, Joseph interpreted the dreams of the two officials accordingly which went ahead to open the door to the King's Palace for him. First, Pharaoh's dream: The Lord caused Pharaoh to dream and no one was able to interpret his Dream. Palace: Joseph was called in to interpret Pharaoh's dreams, the Lord gave him ability to interpret the king's dream.

Divine campaign stand, Joseph never went back to the prison, the Lord had set a Campaign Stand where he did not have to spend money, make empty promises, abuse, or mudsling anyone. The Lord had worked it out for him from the time he started to dream.

12th September 2010

I suggested to Clare and Emmanuel that we start a three day fast for Robert, by Friday no one was concerned about it but I again reminded them that if it is difficult to do it together, let each one separate himself at a time he choses and we do it. Then for me I said I will start over the weekend, but did not do it still yet the Lord was preparing His own timing. 23rd September 2010

Meal for the journey, we suggested to get lunch from Nabukenya, matooke and meat, Clare said she did not want to eat meat and for me I was on delicacy fast for some time. I heard that today you are going to eat that meat; I resisted. The Lord said the command can be do or do not. It can be a Eat or Do Not Eat, so it depends on your obedience to do what you are told to do or what you are told not to do. On the way home I branched at Embassy Super Market bought provision, among them honey and yogurt, when I reached home, I wanted to eat yogurt as I was going not to eat supper after a big Lunch because I was still satisfied. The Spirit said "No, do not eat yogurt," and I left it. Within me I heard a witness saying today's lunch was your meal for the journey. *1ˢᵗ October 2010*

SOLOMON FINISHED PREPARING TO BUILD GOD'S HOUSE, 1 Chronicles 29. Solomon is granted wisdom and knowledge, 2 Chronicles 1. Paul praises and thanks God and the Ephesians, for support, Ephesians 1.

Early in the morning in the kitchen, I heard "Start the Journey." A message came to me that Until the priest's feet touched the water, River Jordan stopped to flow. Remember you are saying that "The most exciting journey will not start until you take the first step."

Before the Commissioning it's me who directs the fast: first, Elijah with the Raven at the Brook, then to the Widow before he went to call fire, to execute the 400 priests of Baal and then call the rain down. Second, John the Baptist, wearing the skins of camels, eating of the locusts and grasshoppers in order to Baptize the one sent from heaven, Jesus Christ. And third, Jesus Christ, 40 days and nights fasting in order to come out with the power to demonstrate God's love to mankind.

Those who take a fast before the Commissioning is "Pre-fast," they are prone to the trap of the evil one, who moves ahead and fulfills the request or desire of their hearts. God does not Call the "Prepared, He Prepares those He has Called" *2ⁿᵈ October 2010*

Gertrude Kabatalemwa with son Emmanuel

CHAPTER ELEVEN

ASK WHAT YOU WANT

I SPENT the day at home.

Message, Be yourself, be natural, be normal and relax. Be my strength each day and my salvation, my prayer, be merciful because I have waited upon you in the time of trouble. Isaiah 33:2. 2 Chronicles 2, Ephesians 2.

Be yourself, be normal. People many times when they are asked to do something start doing what I have not told them to do. It is like when a father tells you to stay around, he has somewhere to send you, you instead of preparing and waiting go and tell him, send me you said you wanted to send me, I am ready send me. How will you father think of you!! Or he tells you after a while I have something to tell you, but you keep going to ask him what you said you wanted to tell me something, tell me now. Your dad may tell you, "I know, I am the one who told you, wait I will tell you when I am ready." 3rd *October 2010*

Message, **Solomon builds the temple, 2 Chronicles 3;**
God has a plan and will strengthen, Ephesians 3
I heard the Spirit saying, "you are still going." 4th October 2010

Message, **In everything you do put God first and He** will direct you and crown your efforts with success. Honour the Lord by giving Him the first part of all your income ... Nothing else compares with wisdom, it gives: A long good life, riches, Have two goals: Wisdom that is knowing, and doing right next is Common sense; do not let them slip away for they fill you with a living energy, they keep you from defeat and disaster ... With them on guard you can sleep without fear of plots of wicked men For the Lord is with you He protects you. Honour, Pleasure and Peace. Proverbs 3:6-26.

But will God really live with men? Why even the heavens of the heavens cannot contain you, how much less this Temple which I have built, 2 Chronicles 6:18.

And I pray that Christ will be more and more at home in your hearts, living in you as you, as you trust Him ... Ephesians 3:17. 6th October 2010

Message, **Then, on the 23RD of the 7TH month, he sent** people home, joyful and happy because the Lord had been good to David and Solomon and to His people Israel, 2 Chronicles 7:10.

Live no longer as unsaved do, for they are blinded and confused. Their closed hearts are full of darkness; they are far away from the life of God because they have shut their minds against Him ... Ephesians 4:17-19.

I GOT A QUESTION, WHAT DO YOU WANT ME TO DO FOR YOU AFTER THIS PREPARATION?

Answers:

1. I ask Wisdom to handle every manner of duty you give me in Nations.
2. Lord, I need control of what I say. I will say only what you allow me to say.
3. Lord, have no extravagant demands. That I will take what comes from your hands when they are cleansed and purified.
4. Lord, that I will ask the guidance of the Holy Spirit in my thoughts, words and when going to take action to lead, guide and direct me.
5. Lord, always to have separate quiet time with you for fellowship: Short time in a day and long for one complete day and a week in a year.
6. Lord, that I may not boast of any accomplished task or battle but always give glory to you.
7. Lord, to continue cultivating my love to greater heights for you.
8. Lord, to lift you in great esteem when presenting you to the great leaders of nations, kings, wise men of the world, richest, religious leaders, multitudes or individuals.

7th October 2010

Message, Solomon followed the instructions of his father David, 2 Chronicles 8:14-15.

The kingdom of Christ and of God will never belong to anyone who is impure or greedy ... talks about darkness and light do not mix ... about wine many evils lie along that path ... befilled with ... Ephesians 5:5-18.

"Ask what you want." Continued from 7th October question.

Answer: 9) Lord, Give me abilities to be myself without imitating others and walk before you in Obedience. *8th October 2010*

LEFT FOR THE VILLAGE.

Message, King Solomon was richer and wiser than all kings on the earth. Kings from every nation came to visit him ... 2 Chronicles 9:22.

The only commandment that ends with a promise; Children obey your ... if you honour your ... yours will be long life full of blessings. Put on God's Armor ... We are not fighting flesh and blood, 13 pieces of God's armor, Ephesians 6:1-18.

Song, Ihe! Ihe! Ihe! Ihe lyomurro x 2 lya baana ba Ruhanga.
My version:
Mukama mpa amani x 2
Mukama mpa amani ndwane na sitani
Mukama mpa Obumanzi - nsigule sitani
Mukama mpa Amagezi - mpakane na sitani
Mukama mpa Omwigo - ntere sitani
Mukama mpa Obumanzi - mbinge sitani

Mukama mpa Omwoyo - anyebere

"Ask what you want." Continued from 7ᵗʰ October question

Answer: 10) Lord, give me ability of clarity in thoughts, words and action that I will not stammer get dry of speech, that the Holy Spirit will be my fountain which does not stop flowing, but keep running. *9ᵗʰ October 2010*

MESSAGE, FOR ME TO LIVE IS CHRIST AND TO DIE, Philippians 1:21. The Lord will turn mourning in to Joy, Jeremiah 31, Isaiah 60, and 2 Chronicles 10. *10ᵗʰ October 2010*

MESSAGE, 2ᴺᴰ CHRONICLES 11, PHILIPPIANS 2

"Ask what you want." Continued from 7ᵗʰ October question

Answer: 11) Lord, give me ability not to reveal the source of my strength, beauty, boldness, youth, wisdom as Samson when he revealed his source that was the end of his strength, but let me sum it up and call it: Obedience and Grace; the Lord is my source of my all in all.

12) May I please, be obedient to the Holy Spirit to lead, guide and direct me as Esther of the old, who was obedient to Hegai who knew what the king wanted in order to be approved as a queen. Hegai knew what pleased the king and supplied her according to the choices of the king desired in a queen, therefore Holy Spirit be the supplier of my every need and want which will please my Lord in this Ministry He has called me. *11ᵗʰ October 2010*

MESSAGE, 2 KINGS 4:23, 2 CHRONICLES 12, PHILIPPIANS 3
Due to exhaustion, the enemy wanted to lie to me, to break. The Lord gave me a message when I Was in the Village: "It is Well," 2 Kings 4:26. *12th October 2010*

LEFT THE VILLAGE FOR KAMPALA.

Message, Be anxious for nothing but in everything by prayer... Philippians 4:6. Proverbs 30, and 2 Chronicles 13.

Song, Amazima nuwe mwebesa, yanyebesa ebyenyuma. (He made me forget the past.)

"Ask what you want." continued from 7th October question

Answer: 13) Cause kings, rulers, wise men, poor, young and old, beggars to approach me and ask questions which will lead me to share with them your mercies and Grace in the area of: Wisdom - spiritually, physically, governance of people and estates. Care for the poor, needy orphans, widows spiritually, physically, materially and financially. Ability to maintain strength, memory, beauty, storage, retreaval for the good cause of the continuancy of the ministry for the service of the Lord. *13th October 2010*

MESSAGE, 2 CHRONICLES 14 AND COLOSSIANS 1.

Song, Nkulindirire Mukama, (I am waiting upon you Lord). *14th October 2010*

Message, Asa had a zeal for the Lord even he removed his mother of a seat of a queen mother because of idolatry. He was perfect for 35 years and experienced no war.

2 Chronicles 15.

Therefore, let no one judge you on the matter of food, drink or in regard to feast days, new moon or Sabbath such things are only the of shadows of the things are to come ... Colossians 2. 15th October 2010

Graduating Class

Kabatalemwa with Mayors of Antelope Valley, CA

CHAPTER TWELVE

BE YOURSELF, BE NATURAL

SONG, Nkulindirire

The Judgment is going to start in the house of the Lord, Ezekiel 9. Asa removed his eyes from the Lord and in the 36th year things changed, 2 Chronicles 16.

God is not a discriminator of persons, Colossians 3 and 4. 16th October 2010

MESSAGE, THEREFORE I WILL REVEAL MY NAME TO MY people and they shall know the power in that name. Then at last, Isaiah 52:6.

The Lord was with Jehoshaphat because he followed in the good footsteps of his father's early years (Asa) ... So the Lord strengthened his position, all people gave taxes, so he became very wealthy, 2 Chronicles 17:3-5

Make the most of your chances to tell others the Good News. Be wise in all your contacts with them, Colossians 4:5-6.

The Love of the Father, It came to my mind that the Lord loves us so much, that at times when He wants to bless us He will go ahead and make a strategy in order to reward us. I liken it to my mum and grand when I was young, about 4 years, I went in the backyard and dug my small garden but my mum came and made it big and planted sweet potatoes and millet there for me and called it Kabatalemwa's garden. Later when the crops were ready she harvested them and rejoiced and told my dad and everybody a bout the greatness of my garden, yet she is the one who dug it.

So, the Love of the Father is like that, when He wants to bless us, He prepares a marathon and gives us all the equipment to finish the race and not only that He leads, guides and directs us in order to reach the finish line. All the way up to the end, when we are through, He is the happiest and goes on to say hurrah! Hurrah!! She and he has done it! And then rewards us as if we were the ones who did it. 17th October 2010

MESSAGE, YOURS, LORD IS THE GREATNESS, POWER, GLORY and ... 1 Chronicles 29:11.

Jehoshaphat asked the king of Israel please inquire first the Word of the Lord ...2 Chronicles 18:4, 34.

For you recall brethren our labour and hardship working day and night among you. Night and day we toiled and sweated to earn ... 1 Thessalonians 2:9. 18th October 2010

MESSAGE, LET US NOT LOOSE HEART IN DOING GOOD FOR IN due time we will reap if we do not grow weary, Galatians 6:9.

Jehu son of Hanani, met Jehoshaphat and said "Should you help the wicked, and love those who hate the Lord ... 2 Chronicles 19:2, 3.

For we speak as messengers from God, trusted by Him to tell the truth; we change his message not one bit to suit the taste ... 1 Thessalonians 2:4. *19th October 2010*

Song, All hail the Power of Jesus Name

Message, about what you eat (Kosher), Canaanite woman, multiplication of 7 loaves and few fish for 4,000 men, Matthew 15:32-37.

Jehoshaphat's prayer, ... his enemies destroyed, ... his alliance with Ahazia displeases God, 2 Chronicles 20:5, 20, 35 and 1 Thessalonians 3, All.

"Ask what you want." Continued from 7th October question

Answer:

14) That my children will know you and serve you with me diligently.

15) Physical and Financial to finish building Primary, Nursery, Multipurpose Hall, Secondary, High school, Teachers quarters, Boarding facilities, Vocational, Health Center and University

16) Purchase of Amber Plots for Bethel Tower, GGT.

17) Own air transport to go to minister to Nations, colour & languages

Be Yourself, Be Natural, The Lord calls those He has prepared and He does not call those who are prepared. You have nothing to add on or contribute when the Lord starts to prepare you for His Ministry it is His duty. You wait, listen and obey to

His instructions. Joseph was in prison doing his cores as usual until when the guards came for him, when the Lord had finished His preparation. He wondered what was taking place when he saw himself being shaved, clothed in fine clothes. Many thoughts went on in his head, until they carried him before Pharaoh to interpret his dream, after that he never went back to the prison.

Mordecai after the fast was going on with his usual business at the Palace gate until when he saw the Palace official Haman asking him to follow him in the palace to cloth him with the kings robes and mount him on the king's horse. He was wondering "What's happening?" He never went back to keep the gate. Queen Esther, Daniel, etc. when they were called to the king never went back to their respective places, but they did not sit and say God, I am going to pray harder, fasting more days, climbing the mountain and spending a week or more there. The Lord had prepared them.

When the Lord has called you for preparation for His Ministry do not put in your flesh, let Him do His work, He does not need your help. Be Yourself, Be Natural Be Normal and Relax and let God do His work in you.

PREPARATIONS DIFFER:

Joseph - was prepared to save his people from starvation

- Suffered the rejection of his brothers
- Bargained and purchased by the highest bidder, Potiphar
- Served in the house of Potiphar as slave
- Persecuted by Potiphar's wife
- Thrown in prison
- Crowed as a Prime Minister of Egypt

Mordecai - was prepared to save the Jews from execution by Haman

- Suffered as a captive from his home land to Susa
- He refused to pay homage to Haman and he suffered the hatred of Haman
- Persecuted by Haman
- A gallow was made to hang him
- His enemy hanged on the gallows and he was crowned as a Prime Minister

John the Baptist – Forerunner of our Lord

- Lived in open fields
- Ate locusts and grasshoppers
- Clothed in camel's hair
- Persecuted by Herod's wife
- His head was cut off and was crowned in heaven.

The Lord has called many people, prepare to them and then sent them to His ministry, but when He calls them they start telling Him send me quickly I am ready to go, and they Commission themselves as Pastors, Apostles, Prophets. Things of the world should teach us things of the spiritual. No Minister or Ambassador appoints himself to a Ministry or Mission. The President announces them and appoints them to a Ministry or Mission Field basing on their education background, qualification and conduct. But in the Lord's Service people appoint themselves with all their flaws.

Many brethren when they get a prophecy, next time you will hear they have gone into a fast of 21 days 40 days preparing themselves. They have no time to wait. They dash into a ministry self commissioned.

When God chooses you there is time He allows you for preparation to sheave you, shift you, strain you and shake every chaff off of you, in order to send a seasoned and cultured ambassador.

If you do not allow time to be prepared, you will go with all that impurities kill yourself and the people of God spiritually, even physically. These days of Internet have created a monster, many Christians are using the web to be considered as elite know how to use computers to solicit for funds to build Churches, orphanages, schools, hospitals, etc. Brother, out there they are are wolves. All fake people are on the look out like GAYs homosexuals, lesbians and satanists name it. There is plenty of money, people who want to come and help, many have fallen into traps. After you giving them your money they ask if you will do them a favour, will you refuse?

One lady said "for me I do not mind who ever gives me money I will take it and ... Let us wait, If the Lord has called us, let us wait for Him to prepare us, so that He can send us." 20th October 2010

CHAPTER THIRTEEN

CALLED OF THE LORD TO BE PREPARED

SONG, Nkulindirire Mukama, I am waiting upon you Lord.

Message, Woe to that one who trust in men, As a lion or the young lion growls over his prey ... and Assyrians will be destroyed, but not by sword of men. The sword of God will smite them. They will ... Isaiah 31. And God will greatly bless his people. Wherever they plant, bountiful crops will spring up, and their flocks and herds will graze in green pastures, Isaiah 33:20.

When Jehoshaphat died he gave the kingship to Jehoram because he was the oldest ... did wrong when he killed all his brothers ... Jehoram was on a binge of doing evil constantly because he had married the daughter of Ahab and Ahab's family became his advisors. Elijah the Prophet wrote him a letter, 2 Chronicles 21.

This would be your ambition: to live a quiet life, minding your own business and doing your own work, just as we told you before, 1 Thessolanians 4:11.

Message,

- You denied yourself comfort; I will reward you before Nations.
- The tears you shed in secret for me! I will give you laughters in the Open.
- You love me so much and left all pleasures of the world! I will show you, everybody, that you are the ones I love.

21st October 2010

MESSAGE, SON OF DUST WEEP FOR THE KING OF TYRE. TELL him, the Lord God says: You were the perfection of wisdom and beauty. You were ... The Lord talks about the beauty of satan before he rebelled and was thrown from Heaven, Ezekiel 28:12. Ahaziah was evil too, his mother encouraged him to do evil, she was called Athaliah of the family of Ahab. God punished Ahaziah because he allied with Jehoram the son of Ahab, he died at a tender age because of wickedness of his maternal uncle's advice. 2 Chronicles 22 .

> *The day of the Lord is coming like a thief.*
> *Dear brothers, you are not in the dark ...*
> *For you are all children of the light ...*
> *So be on your guard, not sleep like the other ...*
> *Night is the time for sleep, and when others get drunk...*
> *But let us who live in the light keep sober...*
> *For God has not chosen to pour out His anger upon us... 1 Thessalonians 5:1-8*

Message, "I have seen the deep sorrow of my people in Egypt, and have heard their pleas ... Exodus 3:7. That is why the Lord has called you, He wants to prepare you. people who are being prepared for a Call, we do not Know what is ahead!!

Those who are called of the Lord to be prepared, do not know until the day of the Commissioning. When the preparation for the call starts there are many questions of Why? When? How?

- Why me? Of all people, I am the one to experience this, circumstance, a situation or a state of affair. Maybe I did not hear well. May be its not the Lord! But the shifting, squeezing, sheaving, straining and winnowing continues.
- When will it stop? Where will it lead me? It seems it's going on and on and on. You wonder!
- How long Lord I am going to keep waiting upon you? Time is running out! I am getting to old to marry, to have a child, to have a house of my own, to have a job remember Abraham on the 100th year he got a child, and remember the story of Hagar.
- Where do I get this strength to bear all this? Abraham lived on until the promise came. Where are you taking me?
- Which place are you sending me? Moses asked! Back to Egypt.
- What am I suppose to tell the Israelites or do? Lead My people out of Egypt.
- What will I tell them if they ask me who sent you? Tell them "God has sent me."
- Who are you? "I AM what I am."

Moses the Patriarch lived in the palace of Pharaoh from the time he was picked on the bank of River Nile. He never suffered lack of any sort, until the day when he tried to help a fellow Israelite and he killed the Egyptian. From that time troubles ensured. Moses had to leave the comfort zone and go to look after the flock of Jethro who later became his father in law.

Imagine the hardship of a herdsman, no shelter when the sun shines or it rains, no food or water, live alone sleep, a man who came from the palace and knew no suffering, but circumstance brought him into this situation. Fourty years he was there living in the wilderness looking after his father-in-laws flocks asking himself:

"Where was I?" In Pharaohs' Palace.

"Where I am now?" In the Wilderness looking after the sheep of Jethro.

"Where am I going?" Only God knows!

Now the time for the Call to go where the Lord had been preparing him in the wilderness came, he had gone through the preparation of 40 years waiting. The trials in the wilderness he encountered in order to be broken down and shaped into a vessel of honour. The Lord had time to break that kingly environment of palace surroundings as he was accustomed in the Pharaoh's palace.

The Commissioning on Mount Horeb (Sinai), the mountain of God Moses saw a flame of fire in a burning bush, and out of the burning bush came a command, Do not come closer and Take off your shoes, Exodus 3:1-6.

Now I am going to send you to Pharaoh, to demand that he let you lead my people out of Egypt. Remembering the terms when he left the palace of Pharaoh, Moses answered "But I am not the person for a job like that. God told him, I will certainly be with you, and this is the proof that I am the one who is sending you; when you have led the people out of Egypt, you shall worship God here upon this mountain. Moses asked, what if the people of Israel ask me which God are you talking about? God replied, The Sovereign God, I AM has sent me! Jehovah, the God of your ancestors, Exodus 3:10-14.

Moses insisted, they will not believe me!" God asked Moses "What do you have there in your hand?"

After 40 years of preparation in the wilderness the Lord gave Moses the tools: a) the Rod he used to cause Miracles, and Aaron to be your spokesman, the Lord appointed him an Assistant, Exodus 4:1-17.

When God is saying "Go," there is no need for you to say "No" or "buts" in our relationship to God's will. Nothing will take the Lord by surprise, when He says "Go," He knows it's you to do it when He asked whom can I send, you said: here I am send me Lord, Isaiah 6:8, and He said, I will send you Every provision had been made for the appointed task. The Lord says, I will not fail Thee.

> He who gives the command will also give the equipment.
>
> JOHN HENRY JOWETT

After preparing you when the Lord is sending you He does not send you empty handed, He gives you start up capital, Exodus 3:22. And I will give these people favour and respect in the sight of the Egyptians; and it shall be that when you go, you shall not go empty handed. Exodus 3:21. But every woman shall insistently solicit of her neighbor... The Israelites took all the riches of Egypt when they left, gold, silver, finest of clothes, etc. You will clothe your sons and daughters with the best of Egypt.

The Lord will also kill all those enemies who wanted to kill you, Exodus 4:19. The Lord said to Moses in Midian, Go back to Egypt for all the men who were seeking your life are dead. 22nd October 2010

CHAPTER FOURTEEN

THE LORD IS FAITHFUL, HE WILL MAKE YOU STRONG

MESSAGE, Exodus 1 – 4, Repeated it.

The Priest Jehoiada did a great act by executing Athaliah, a wicked grandchild of Ahab, from the throne of Judah which was promised to David and his ancestors and restored his grandchild Joash, 2 Chronicles 23.

And they speak of how you are looking forward to the return of God's son from heaven, Jesus, whom God brought back to life and He is our only salvation from God's terrible anger against sin, 2 Thessolonians 1:10. 23rd October 2010

THEN JESUS WAS LED OUT INTO THE WILDERNESS BY THE Holy Spirit, ... Jesus returned home ... when He heard that John was arrested. He moved besides Lake Galilee. Matthew 5:1-13.

Jesus went everywhere preaching the Good News about the Kingdom of Heaven, and healed every kind of sickness and disease. Matthew 5:23.

Zechariah, Johoiada's son, warned King Joash and he was

paid by the king killing him, forgetting that even the throne he was sitting on was the effort of Johoiada. Zechariah's last words were "Lord, see what they are doing and pay them back." 2 Chronicles 24:20.

The Anti-Christ will be revealed and the Lord Jesus will slay him with ... The coming of the lawless one is through working of satan and will be attended by great lying wonders and miracles ... With all wicked deception for those who are perishing ... Therefore, God sends upon them a misleading influence ... 2 Thessalonians 2:8-11.

Message, The principle of Prison on the earth is of reducing on the sentence when you behave well 50 years become 25 years. But in the Heavenly kingdom principles there is multiplication factor. The trials you go through the reward is multiplied 20 years of suffering becomes 40 years of reward. 24th October 2010

WHEN YOU FIRST EXECUTE TRUE JUDGMENT AND SHOW mercy and kindness and tender compassion, every man to his brother, oppress not the widow or fatherless ... So it came to pass that as He cried and they would not hear. He said: So they shall cry and I will not answer, says the Lord of Hosts. Zechariah 7:8-13, Isaiah 58.

If you deal with people who are not with God or who are enemies of God, the Lord will not defeat your enemies no matter how well you Fight for God has power to help or to frustrate, 2 Chronicles 25:7.

"Ask what you want." continued from 7th **October question**

Answer: 18) Lord, always choose for me people to work with who fear your name and are your friends.

King Amaziah after conquering the Edomites he brought their idols and worshipped them. The Lord was so angry and sent a prophet to ask Amaziah "Why have you worshipped idols who could not even save their own people from you?" Chronicles 25:14-15.

The Lord is Faithful, He will make you Strong and Guard you from satanic attacks of every kind. ... Stay away from a Christian who spends his days in laziness and does not follow the ideal of hard work we set up for you ... Even while we were still there with you, we gave you this rule "He who does not work shall not eat." 2 Thessalonians 3:3-10.

Teaching of the True Church on Hi Pop Cult, Why do people follow those who are godless, like Gospel Singers teaming with secular worldly musicians?

The fallen angels, Bene ha Elohim is the name of fallen angels un Job 2 and Jude 1:6.

The Lord destroyed the world with a flood because of the fallen angels who came and started sleeping with women on earth and produced half angel and half being called giants, Nephilim, which is the name for giants who were 30 feet tall. The Lord caused the flood to drawn these giants. Noah survived because he was the only one who had uncorrupted blood line with the fallen angels, Genesis 6 and 9. Now after the flood the nephilim giants bodies we destroyed but the spirits went back to their houses, Luke 11:24.

Corruption started from two people: Nimrod and Semiramis, wife mother of Nimrod, their child was Ninas. That is where we see the Catholics with Mother and a Child Worship (Cult). When Nimrod died his body was cut into 14 pieces but later one was missing of the penis (obelisk), so they got 13 pieces. Egyptian religion of tall statues, a half pyramid with an Eye is from Babylon, this unfinished pyramid is the Tower of Nimrod and the eye of false knowledge. Demons, up to now, wants to become superior to human beings, but Jesus gave us the Power and Authority over them, John 17:22. The Lord created Israel nation to Fight corruption of the Nephilim spirits. Amalekites who were defeated by Israelites were giants. Joshua Fought a war with the tribes of giants but Acan betrayed them by taking what was forbidden by the Lord. So, they were defeated because evil cannot Fight with evil. An open eye called "All Seeing" on the unfinished tower of Babylon looks like a pyramid. That in 2012 year, that is when Nimrod will be coming to complete his tower of Babylon. Satanists were anxiously waiting, but it was not come. *25th October 2010*

CHAPTER FIFTEEN

WAITING FOR HIS BRIDE

HEAR NOW what the Lord is saying. Arise, plead your case before the mountains and let the hills hear your voice. Listen you mountains, to the indictment of the Lord. Any you enduring foundation of the earth because the Lord has a case against His people; even with Israel He will dispute. My people what have I done to you and how have I wearied you? Answer me. ... The Lord require of you; To do justice, to love kindness, and walk humbly with your God, Micah 6:1-3, 8.

Uzzaih when he became strong, his heart was so proud that he acted corruptly, and he was unfaithful to the Lord his God, for he entered the temple of the Lord to burn incense on the altar of incense. ... As he was arguing with the priests the leprosy broke on his forehead before the priests in the house of the Lord beside the altar of incense, 2 Chronicles 25:16-19.

For God has not given us a spirit of fear, timidity, but of power and love and discipline.

Therefore, do not be ashamed of the testimony of our Lord or of me I His prisoner but join with me in suffering for the gospel ... 1 Timothy 1:7-9.

Prayer, Wherever you are taking me save me from pride, which has many of your servants to fall from the grace. Your servant Moses even though he had to lead all the children of Israel he was the humblest. Even though Joseph was exalted to the seat of the Prime Minister of Egypt, he was down to the earth because he knew whatever he had was from you. Save me from self-exaltation, use me as your mouth piece, thus speak when I am to speak and be quiet when I am to be quiet. Save me from eating too much, your servants have been bribed with food, they eat and became sick. Lord, cause my eyes to see what you want me to see, and close them if there is anything you do not want me to see. Keep my heart from wanting for more, let me be contented with what you provide for me. Lord tap on my shoulder whenever there is danger before me and warn me of evil people who come dressed in sheep's skin. Give me ability to learn from You daily and interpret situations as the Holy Spirit leads. Amen. 26th October 2010

Message, Woe to my rebellious children, says the Lord; you ask advice from everyone but me, and decided to do what I do not want you to do. You yoke yourselves with unbelievers, thus piling up your sins... See them moving slowly across the terrible desert to Egypt donkeys and camels laden down with treasure to pay for Egypt's aid. On through the badlands they go, where lions, viper and flying serpents. They will give you nothing in return. For their promises are worthless! "The reluctant dragon" I call her! Isaiah 30:1-6.

For they are stubborn rebels they tell my prophets. "Shut up we do not want any more of you reports" Or they say, "Do not tell us the truth; tell us nice things, tell us lies. Forget all this gloom we've heard more than enough about your Holy One of Israel and all he says, Isaiah 30:10-11.

This is the reply of the Holy one of Israel; because you despised what I tell you and trust in frauds and lies and won't repent, therefore, calamity will come upon you suddenly, as a upon a bulging wall that bursts and falls, in one moment it comes crashing down. God will smash you like a potter's jar, He will not act sparingly. So ruthlessly shattered that a shard (Oruguhyo) will not be found among its pieces to take fire from a hearth (mukyoto) or to scoop water from a cistern (Iziba). Isaiah 30: 12.

Even though the Lord promises salvation and peace and strength. You say "No we will get our help from Egypt; they will give us swift horses for riding to battle." But the only swiftness you are going to see is the swiftness of your enemies chasing you! Is. 30:14-5.

Yet the Lord still waits for you to come to Him so He can show you His love; He will conquer you to bless you, just as He said. For the Lord is faithful to His promises. Blessed are all those who wait for Him to help them, Isaiah 30:18

King Jotham became powerful because he was careful to follow the path of the Lord his God, 2 Chronicles 27:6.

So, I want men everywhere to pray with holy hands lifted up to God, free from sin and anger and resentment. And the women should not over paint themselves , not with elaborate hair arrangement or gold or pearls should be at the same quiet and sensible in manner of dressing, 1 Timothy 2:8-10.

Prayer, Lord, where you taking me let me not crash, let the Holy Spirit be the one to pilot my airbus in space. Lord, let me not sink, let the Holy Spirit be the one guide my big ship of my life through the shallow and deep waters. Lord, let me not derail, let the Holy Spirit be the one to be the driver of my long train on those steel rails. Lord, let me not overturn, let the Holy Spirit be the driver of my semi truck along the narrow roads, dusty, potholed, corners, ascending and descending steep hills.

Song, Jesus bowed down and died looking at me. When I was chained and in Prison, and deep in the grave He said "its over, the chains were broken. The prison's gate opened and the power of the grave gave me up. Lord Jesus, I am on my knees to say thank you!!! I am here on my knees to worship you. Lifting up my hands Where would I be if Jesus did not come? I would be dead in transgression, O! what a shame for my soul!! Now He is waiting for me in heaven above. Dressed in splendor and smiling, waiting for His bride!! 27th *October* 2010

CHAPTER SIXTEEN

THE LORD DOES NOT STAND REBELLION

KING DARIUS APPOINTED 3 COMMISSIONERS, Daniel was one. Then Daniel distinguished himself among the commissioners and straps because he possessed an extraordinary Spirit and the king planned to appoint him over the entire kingdom. Then the commissioners and satraps started to find ground of accusation against Daniel in regard to government affairs but could not find no ground of accusation in as much as he was faithful, and no negligence or corruption was to be found in him. Then they agreed to find any ground of accusation against him with regard to the law of his God.

They spoke to the king that he should establish a statute and enforce an injunction that anyone who makes petition to any god or man besides you, O king for thirty days, shall be cast into the lions' den, now O! king sign.

When Daniel heard that the decree was signed, went as usual to his roof chamber window open towards Jerusalem knelt down and worshipped his God. These men came and found Daniel making petition and supplication before his God. They ran to the king to accuse him mentioning that this exile from Judah pays no attention to you, O! king, by mentioning exile from Judah they wanted to arouse the king's anger. The king was deeply distressed and set his mind on delivering Daniel until sunset he kept exerting and excusing himself to rescue him. These men insisted that the law of the Medes and Persians or statutes may not be changed. The king at last gave orders and Daniel was brought in and cast into the Lions' den. The king spoke to Daniel and prayed for him, and in The king went off to his palace and started fasting for him no food no any Form of entertainment. They rose at dawn, at the break of the day and went in haste to the lions' den and call out with a troubled voice ... Daniel answered him ... The king gave order, and they brought those men with their children and wives ... The king made a decree that in all the dominion of his kingdom men are to fear and tremble before the God of Daniel, Daniel 6. *28th October 2010*

MESSAGE, BECAUSE OF THE PRIDE OF KING ZEDEKIAH, WHEN prophet Jeremiah advised him to surrender and he refused to surrender, Jeremiah 29:17-19, the king of Babylon made Zedekiah watch as they killed his children and all the nobles of Judah, then gouged out his eyes, bound him in chains and sent him away to Babylon as a slave.

Always God cares for His Servants, king Nebuchadnezzar had told his officials to find Jeremiah. "See that he isn't hurt" he said look after him well and give him everything he wants. ... They sent soldiers to bring Jeremiah out of the prison, and put him into the care of Gedaliah to take him back to his home. Jeremiah 39:11.12

King Hezekaiah his rule was a good one in the Lord's opinion, just as his ancestor David's had been. He reopened the doors of the Temple and repaired them. He summoned the priests and the Levites, He organized Levites at the Temple into an Orchestral group, using cymbals, psalteries, and harps. This was in accordance with the directions of David and the prophets Gad and Nathan who had received their instructions from the Lord. 2 Chronicles 29:25-26.

But the Spirit distinctly and expressly declares that in later times some will fall away from the faith, paying attention to deceitful spirits and doctrines of demons... For everything created by God is good and nothing is to be rejected if it is received with gratitude, for it is sanctified by means of the word of God and prayer... Do not waste time arguing over foolish ideas and silly myths and legends. Spend your time and energy in the exercise of keeping spiritually fit. Bodily exercise is all right, but spiritually exercise is much more important and is a tonic for all you do. So, exercise yourself spiritually and practice being a better Christian, because that will help you not only now in this life, but in the next life too, 1 Timothy 4:1-8. 29th October 2010

THE SPIRIT OF THE LORD DOES NOT STAND REBELLION. When rebellion takes over the Spirit of the Lord leaves, and the tormenting spirit comes. But the Spirit of the Lord had left Saul, and instead, the Lord sent a tormenting spirit that filled him with depression and fear.

Singing Praises to the Lord is a cure, Saul's aids suggested to bring a harpist and David's name was suggested as he was the only talented harp player, handsome, brave, strong and had good spirit as well as solid judgment, 1 Samuel 16:14-18.

David was the youngest son and was on Saul's staff on a part time basis. He went back and forth to Bethlehem ... One day

Jesse said to David "take this bushel of roasted grain and these ... to your brothers. Never judge any body by age, size, education, etc. But when David's oldest brother Eliab, heard David talking like that he was angry.

"What are you doing around here, any way"... I know what a cocky brat you are... David said "Do not you worry about a thing I will take care of this Philistine." Saul said "how can a kid like you Fight with a man like him,You are only a boy and he has been in the army since he was a boy!" David insisted ... Saul blessed him. When the heathen or ungodly swear by their idols. You Declare or swear by the Living God, David shouted in reply, "You come to me with a sword and a spear, but I come to you in the name of the Lord of the armies of heaven and Israel - the very God whom you have defied. Today the Lord will conquer you and I will kill you and cut off your head; and then I will ... The stone sunk in and the giant man fell on his face to the ground. Since he had no sword he ran over ... Samuel 17.

God will give you ability to kill your enemies with their own weapons, e.g. witchcraft, guns, etc.

King Hezekiah Honours the Lord with prayer and causes all Judah and some tribes of Israel to be blessed, 2 Chronicles 30:18-21.

Never speak sharply to an older man, but plead with him respectfully just as though he were your own father. Talk to... Treat all older women as mothers... Pastors who do their work well should be paid well and should be highly appreciated... Do not listen to complaints against the pastor unless there are... If he has really signed, then he should be rebuked in front of the whole church so that no one else will follow his example, 1 Timothy 5:1-20.

On this 29th day of my journey as I was praying in the morning, Prayers again when the Holy Spirit asked me: **"Ask what you want." continued from 7th October question.**

About Answer: 8) As I was reading my journals all these years the Lord was asking me "What do you want me to do for you? After sitting and asking myself that I have asked all what I wanted the Lord to do for me, but why does He insist on that question. Maybe I have never answered His question. Lord, give me strength to finish in power, this journey you have called me to take. 30th October 2010

Gertrude Kabatalemwa created and taught the women to make Kasoya Dolls to help raise funds for the school

First Classroom with wood and sticks

Primary Class in 2006

CHAPTER SEVENTEEN

AKANGONZA YESU AKANGONZA

Prayer, Lord, give me nations to reach them for you!!!

LORD, let all the gifts and fruits of the Holy Spirit surround me for all my life as long as I live.

Lord, give me a break-through spiritually: because it is you who gave me the Holy Spirit to minister unto you and this Spirit is yours and it will return to you. Lord, give me a break-through physically because you gave me this body for the housing of my Soul and your Holy Spirit to minister through this physical body unto you, use the wisdom, knowledge, understanding, beauty and good health you have given me to reach all continents of the Universe.

Lord, give me a breakthrough financially because all the riches in this world belongs to you and you give it to who pleases you. These riches are to enhance your Kingdom on this earth by ministering to Your people.

Lord, whatever you give me materially let them be land, ships, gold, silver, diamonds, estates, skyscrapers, planes, fleets of vehicles, money, let them be for your service, that I will return them to you to do your Will through me by ministering life eternal to your people.

Lord, I command whatever talent you created in me, and the richest people of this world to give unreservedly to me to reach and possess nations and continents of this world for your glory.

When all these come to pass, let me live, walk and use them faithfully up to the last breath when I meet you in Glory.

Lord, let me not continue arguing with you, as I have avoided this issue and have fought it nail and tooth, but now I surrender!!! Give me your Heart's choice of a companion you have prepared for me from the beginning of the world. Amen.

I learnt from the teaching on Emma's video: God put enmity between the serpent and the woman and her off spring and the serpents who will bruise and tread his head under foot, and you will lie in wait and bruise his heel, Genesis 3:15.

Jesus Christ was the seed of a woman, because He had incorruptible blood. It's only His blood which was clean after Adam and Eve rebelled against God and God cursed them. So, everyone was born with that curse; until Jesus was to come and offer His pure blood which was not corrupted. 21st July 2011

HEZEKIAH, A MAN OF GOD... WITH HIS OFFICERS, AND mighty men, He stopped the waters of the fountain... He encouraged his people, be strong and courageous be not afraid or dismayed before the king of Syria... With him is an army of flesh, but with us is the Lord, our God, to help us and Fight our battle... Never boast before the war, Sennacherib boasted so much but... For this cause Hezekiah the king and the prophet Isaiah prayed and cried into the Lord of heaven. The Lord sent an angel who destroyed all Syrian officers and generals in the Camp. So the kind of Syria returned shamed faced to his own land. Many people brought gifts to Jerusalem and presents to the Hezekiah king of Judah. And king Hezekiah was magnified in the sight of all nations. Hezekiah got very sick to the point of death; and he prayed to the Lord and He healed him, but Hezehiah did not make returns to the Lord according to the benefits done to him... Hezekiah was a good man he realized his mistake and humbled himself for the pride of his heart, and the wrath of the Lord did not come upon him and the nations. Hezekiah had very great wealth and honour and made for himself treasuries, 2 Chronicles 32:3-27.

For God did not give us the spirit of timidity or fear, but He has given us a spirit of power nd love and calm and well-balanced mind and discipline and self-control. Jesus annulled death the power of the grave and made it of no effect and brought life and immortality, immunity from eternal death to light through the Gospel, 2 Timothy 1:7, 10.

Early in the morning after prayers the Lord gave me a song.
"Akangonza Yesu Akangonza – Jesus Loved me to the end"
Akangonza Yesu Akangonza Jesus Loved me to the end
Akangoza Omuzaire Akangonza He loved me O! king He loved me
Akangonza Omurungi Akangonza Shepherd He loved me
Akangonza Omuliisa Akangonza!! O! sweet Jesus He loved me!!!

Yesu yaroozire nyowe okufa When He saw me perishing
Akaleka byoona uwe aije afe He came down to die for me
Aheeeeyo obwomezi bwe Gave His life for me
Nyooowe nukwo nkiiireee!! That I may live!!!

Nyowe akaba asibirwe enjegere In chains I was bound!!!
    Ndi mukihanga kyokufa In the valley of death
    Mumitehimbwa yenkomo In the prison's bars
    Yaija yansuumurra!!! He came and set me free!!

Hati Yesu nuwe muliisa wange Now He is my shepherd
    Ntwara habunyansi oburungi He takes me to green pastures
    Anywisa amaizi agatekere And still water!!!
    Agarra omwoyo gwange My soul returns!!!!

Bambi Yesu aliyo andindirize My savior now is waiting for me
    Habwokuba uwe akanihiza As He promised me!!!
    Ati ndigaruka nkutwale That He'll come take me home
    Oikale Nanya ebiro byoona!!! Where He is! I will be!!!
    1st November 2010

CHAPTER EIGHTEEN

CONSIDER YOUR WAYS!

KING MANASSEH WAS evil at first but when the Lord brought the host of Assyrian army and they took him in fetters, then he realized and repented in Babylon. God heard him and brought him back to his kingdom and he stopped worshiping idols and became a good man, 2 Chronicles 33:1-20

Paul was in prison for the Gospel and gave Timothy advice to teach and give instructions to others to teach the gospel ... and Take your share of suffering and hardships which you are called to endure as a good soldier of Jesus Christ. No soldier when in service gets entangled in the enterprises of civilian life, his aim is to satisfy and please the one who enlisted him, and if anyone enters competitive games, he is not crowned unless he completes lawfully, fairly, according to the rules laid down. It is the hard-working farmer who labors to produce who must be the first partaker of the fruit.

If we have died with him, we shall also live with him. If we endure, we shall also reign with him. If we deny and disown and reject Him, He will also deny and disown and reject us. If we are faithless or do not believe and are untrue to Him, He remains true and faithful to His Word and His righteous for he cannot deny Himself. But in a great house there are not only vessels of gold and silver, but also of wood and earthen war, and some for honourable and noble use, and some for menial and daily use. So, whoever, cleanses himself from what is ignoble and unclean, who separates himself from contact with contaminating and corrupting influences will then himself a vessel set apart and useful for honourable and noble purpose, consecrated and profitable to the Master. Shun youthful lusts and flee from them ... 2 Timothy 2:2-22.

2nd November 2010

The Edomites were so cruel to the Israelites and the Lord was not happy with them. So the Lord cautioned them: You are proud because you live in those high, inaccessible cliffs and you say "who can ever reach us way up here?" Do not fool yourselves says the Lord!

Though you soar as high as eagles and build your nest among the stars, I will bring you plummeting down says the Lord! In that day not one wise man will be left in all of Edom ... For I will fill the wise men of Edom with stupidity. The mightiest, great soldiers of Teman will be confused. All this will happen because of what you did to your brother Israel. You deserted Israel in his time of need. You stood aloof, refusing to lift a finger to help him. You made yourselves rich at his expense.

You stood at the crossroads and killed those trying to escape; you captured the survivors and returned them to their enemies in that terrible time of his distress. The Lord judges the nations that made Israel suffer: The Lord's vengeance will soon fall upon all Gentile nations. As you have done to Israel, so will it be done to you! Your acts will boomerang upon your heads. Obadiah.

Josiah's reign was good as he carefully followed the good example of his ancestor king David. He broke the altars of baal and obelisks... One day when the scroll of the commandments of Moses was found in the temple he rend his garments in humility and the Lord counted it on him... The Lord was going to punish Israel for they had forsaken Him. But the Lord had pity on Josiah when He said: Because you are sorry and have humbled yourself before God when you heard my words against this city and its people, I have heard you, says the Lord and I will not send the promised evil upon this city and its people until after your death, 2 Chronicles 34:14, 24, 27.

In the last days it is going to be very difficult to be a Christian. For people will love themselves and their money they will be proud and boastful sneering at God, disobedient to their parents, ungrateful to them and thoroughly bad. They will be rough and cruel, and sneer at those who try to be good. They will betray their friends, they will be hotheaded, puffed up with pride, and prefer good times rather than worshiping God. They will go to Church but they won't really believe anything they hear. Do not be taken in by people like that ... Yes, and those who decide to please Christ Jesus by living Godly lives will suffer at the hands of those who hate Him, 2 Timothy 3. 3rd *November 2010*

MESSAGE, THIS IS A MESSAGE FROM HAGGAI TO ZERUBBABEL the governor of Judah. And to Joshua the son of Josedech, the high priest saying: Thus says the Lord of hosts, this people says, the time has not come, even the time for the house of the Lord to be rebuilt. Is it time for you yourselves to dwell in your paneled houses while my house lies in desolate?

Now therefore, thus says the Lord of hosts. Consider your

ways! You have sown much, but will harvest little, you eat, but there is not enough to be satisfied; you drink but there is not enough to become drunk; you put on clothing, but no one is warm enough and he who earns, earns wages to put into a purse with holes, Haggai 1.

The Lord was telling the people of Israel that when His house is lying in desolate for while them were sleeping in well built houses, He told them that even if they sow much but they will harvest little. When you think of yourself all the time you do not give for the work of God always there will be lack, you work and work but you will not have enough food, money, clothing.

People have gone to Dubai, when they are there, they tell them that now money is in Hong Kong, when they are in Hong Kong, they tell them money is in Bangkok (Bifuna kiraru). You travel from one city to another but you do not make ends meet. Why? Because you have forgotten the Lord who is your provider, in strength, wisdom your protector where ever you travel so that you do not crash in planes, even He is the one who gives you the breath of life.

People have become heartless, they leave their babies who are still suckling in day care to go after money. They take their children into boarding schools in order to get freedom and go on shopping spree, and their children grow as caged animals in a zoo, they grow without morals because they meet different characters there.

The Lord went further to tell them that: he who earns, earns wages to put into a purse of with holes. True, when you ignore the Lord's house or work; the time you make a good sale that is; when your car smashes another and you have to pay for both the repairs of yours and the one you knocked. Or That day that is when they will tell you, your mother, father, wife, or child is very sick, and that day that is when your cows in the village have been struck by lightning, or that day that is when the Owino market burns, and you forgot to take to the bank the loan or that is when you hear that people have confiscated the plot you gave as a security for the loan. You look for much, but behold it comes to little when you bring it home, and I blow it away, 2 Chronicles 35. 4th November 2010

CHAPTER NINETEEN

THE GRACE AND SMILE OF MY GOD

JOSIAH'S SON Jehoahaz was so evil he reign for only three months and his brother Eliakim named Jehoiakim replaced him but also he was evil and was exiled to Babylon by Nebuchadnezzar. His son Jehoiachin became a king for three and ten days, also he was so evil. His son Zedekiah took over also he was evil... The Lord used the king of Babylon to destroy the Israelites completely. At times the Lord can use ungodly people to punish a nation or His people when they rebel for example Nebuchadnezzar, Idi Amin, etc.

Those who survived exile were taken away to Babylon as slaves to the king and his sons until the kingdom of Persia conquered Babylon. 2 Chronicles 36. Thus the word of the Lord spoken through Jeremiah came true, that the land must rest for seventy years to make up for the years when the people refused to observe the Sabbath. Jeremiah 25:11, Daniel 9:2

Paul left Titus to help strengthen the Church at Crete and to appoint pastors. The men you choose must be well thought of for their good lives, they must have only one wife and their children must love the Lord and not have a reputation of being wild or disobedient to their parents. These pastors must be men of blameless lives because they are God's ministers. They must not be drunkards or Fighters or greedy for money. They must enjoy to welcome visitors... A person who is pure of heart sees goodness; but a person whose own heart is evil and untrusting finds evil in everything, for his dirty mind and rebellious heart color all he sees and hears. Titus 1:1-15. 5th November 2010

I LISTENED AND SAW A VIDEO OF A BRO EXPLAINING THE Nephilim Spirits, Gen 6:4, he said the Lord put His Seed in the Woman. The incorruptible Seed, Jesus Christ, In Genesis He was cursing a snake saying the seed of a woman will bruise his head. So, when Jesus came, He gave us power over Satan, and when we get born-again we get a transfusion of the Blood of Jesus which the devil cannot play with. It is incorruptible Blood of the Lamb of God. You go in with a cringed face and you come out smiling. There are still many people who are saved but they have never experienced Joy. They get joy only moments when they are at church, the moment they leave the brethren, the devil says Aha! come back to me. Until when you are born-aogain that is when you experience full Joy whether brethren are there or not.

I will not die beneath the anger of my God! I will live and die beneath the Grace and smile of my God. Before the mountains were created, before the earth was formed, you are God without beginning or end. You speak, and man turns back to dust. A thousand years are but as yesterday to you! They are like a single hour. We glide along the tides of time as swiftly as a racing river, and vanish as quickly as a dream. We are like grass that is green in the morning but mowed down and withered before the evening shadows fall.

Seventy years are given us! And some may live on to eighty.

But even the best of these years are often emptiness and pain, soon they disappear and are gone. Who can realize the terror of your anger Lord? Which one of use can fear you as he should? Teach us to number our days and recognize how few they are; help us to spend them as we should. Give us gladness in proportion to our former misery! Replace the evil years with good. Let us see your Miracles again; let our children see glorious things and let the Lord our God favor us and give us success, Psalm 90.

God favored Cyrus so much he is the one who overthrew the Babylon Empire, Ezra 1. God moved Cyrus and used him mightily, Isaiah 45:1- 2, to declare that: Cyrus, king of Persia, hereby announces that Jehovah, the God of heaven who gave me my vast empire, has not given me the responsibility of building Him a temple in Jerusalem, in the land of Judah." Psalm 90:7.

Message, The Lord gave me Isaiah 45:2-7, 13, 14 on 1st January 1986 when I was fasting and praying for the rebels of Museveni to come soon and safe. The Lord swears by Himself because there is not any other above him. "Let all the world look to me for salvation! For I am God: there is no other, I have sworn by myself and I will never go back on my word for it is true that every knee in all the world shall bow to me, and every tongue shall swear allegiance to my name." Isaiah 45:22. The Lord swore by Himself that "I have sworn by my great name," Jeremiah 44:26.

Paul again was giving Titus instructions on how to conduct himself, how to treat the elders, older women, youth and pastors, e.g. he instructed Titus in the same way, urge the young men to behave carefully, taking life seriously and there you, yourself, must be an example to them of good deeds of every kind. Your conversation should be so sensible and logical that anyone who wants to argue will be ashamed of himself because there won't be anything to criticize in anything you say. Titus 2:6-8. *6th November 2010*

CHAPTER TWENTY

I HAVE YOUR NAME IN MY SECRET HEART

MESSAGE, I am with you to the End. "I have your name in my Secret Heart."

Let us be glad and rejoice and honour him, for the time has come for the wedding banquet of the Lamb, and His bride has prepared herself. She is permitted to wear the cleanest and whitest and finest of linens. This Fine Linen represents the good deeds done by the people of God. Blessed are those who are invited to the wedding feast of the Lamb. And He added "God Himself has stated this. He was clothed with garments dipped in the blood and His title was 'The Word of God.' The armies of heaven, dressed in finest linen, white and clean, followed him on white horses. Revelation 19:7-9, 13,14

When the enemies of Judah and Benjamin heard that the exiles had returned and were rebuilding the Temple, they approached Zerubbabel and the other leaders and suggested, "Let us work with you, for we are just as interested in your God as you are."

Whenever our enemies understand that we have returned to the Lord or are making progress they want to join us not for good intentions though but they always want to undermine you. They want to find out where you draw your stand, your strength, and your power.

Then Zerubbabel and Jeshua and other Jewish leaders told them No you may have no part in this work. The Temple of the God of Israel must be built by the Israelis as king Cyrus has commanded. Their enemies tried to discourage and frighten them by sending agents to tell lies about them to king Cyrus. Ezra 4:1-3. Yes, when you reject them to build with you; they will try and discourage you, lie against you and frighten you.

God spoke in many different ways to his prophets e.g. dreams, visions, revelations, face to face etc. But now He has spoken to us through His Son Jesus Christ whom He has given everything and through whom he made the world and everything there in. God's Son shines out with God's glory, and all that God's Son is and does marks Him as God. He regulates the universe by the mighty power of His command. He is the one who died to cleanse us and clear our record of all sin, and then sat down in highest honour beside the great God of heaven. God also called Him 'Lord' when He said Lord, in the beginning You made the earth, and the heavens are the work of Your hands. ... And did God ever say to an angel, as He does to His Son, "sit here beside Me in honour until I crush all Your enemies beneath Your feet," Hebrews 1:1-3, 10, 13. 9th *November 2010*

MESSAGE, SUPPOSE I SAY YOU CONTINUE FOR ANOTHER 5 days to take care of some other issues; I complained Lord, it is too ... aha! Ok, 3 days, complaints here and there of weakness but then I said Lord, I am a pot and you are the potter.

40th day; He pointed at me the case of Abraham while on the way with Isaac; is it true Lord that this is from you? Up to the last hour the Lord showed Himself by a provision of a ram.

Question, Does the devil give strength? "No!" Does he create? "No!" he just tears down etc. So, if you knew what I am going to accomplish you would wish that, at least, if you went with me for 80 days. But every day you take it is doubled. On the 13th I left for the village and continued, Saturday 13, Sunday 14, Monday 15, and finished in the morning on Tuesday 16th. What a victory. Wednesday 17th, Sis Judi sent me a text that she would send me an email because she cannot tell it on the phone.

Sound the alarm in Jerusalem, Let the blast of the warming trumpet be heard upon my holy mountain. Let everyone tremble in fear ...In the day of darkness and gloom of black clouds and thick darkness ... What mighty army ... How great, how powerful these people ... Fire goes before them ... They look like tiny horses and they run as fast ... Look at them ... The Lord leads them with a shout. This is his mighty army and they follow his orders. They day of the judgment of the Lord is an awesome, terrible thing. Who can endure it? That is why the Lord says "Turn to me now, while there is time. Give me all your hearts. Come with fasting, weeping, mourning. Let your remorse tear at your hearts and not your garments. Return to the Lord your God for he is gracious and merciful. He is not easily angered; he is full of kindness and anxious not to punish you. Who knows? Perhaps ... I will remove these armies from the north and send them far away. I will return them back into the parched wastelands where they will die, half shall be driven into the Dead Sea and the rest into the Mediterranean, and then their rotting stench will rise upon the land. The Lord has done mighty miracles for you. Fear not my people, be glad now and rejoice, for he has done amazing things for you. He forget not flocks and herds their hunger ... Rejoice ... After I have poured out my rains *again*, I will pour out my SPIRIT upon all of you! Your sons and daughters will prophesy; your old men will dream dreams, and your young men see visions. And I will pour out my Spirit even on your slaves, men and women alike. Joel 2:1-29.

Haggai and Zechariah, the prophets, encouraged the temple building to continue, also they helped in building. But these heathens and their governor continued harassing them asking them who gave permission to rebuild the Temple and finish these walls? and also asked for the list of names of those who were working on the Temple. But because the Lord was overseeing the entire situation, our enemies did not force us ... If the Lord is on Our Side Who Can Be Against Us? King Darius stood on the side of God's people.

That since the messages from angels have been proved true and people denied them and have been punished for disobeying them, what makes us think that we will escape? We are again different to this great message of salvation announced by the Lord Jesus himself and passed on to us by those who walked, talked and slept with Him. God always has shown us that these messages are true ... and has assigned such gifts to each of us. The future world is not going to be controlled by the angels. Hebrew 2:2-16.

What is mere man that you are so concerned about him? And Who is this son of man you honour so highly?

You him lower than the angels for a while and now you have crowned him with Honour and glory. You have put him in complete charge of everything there in. Nothing is left out. Psalm 8.

But we do see Jesus ... and we who have been made holy by Jesus now have the same Father he has in Brotherhood ... We who have been made holy by Jesus, now have the same Father he has.

Brotherhood: That is why Jesus is not ashamed to call us his brothers.

For the word says in Psalms I will talk to my brothers about God my Father, and together we will sing His praises. I will put my trust in God along with my brothers, See, here am I and the children God gave me. Since we, God's children, are human beings made of flesh and blood he became flesh and blood too by being born as a human being so he could die and in dying break the power of the devil who had the power of death. We all know he did not come as an angel but ... Hebrew 2:2-16.

I CAME BACK TIRED AND WENT TO SLEEP RIGHT AWAY AT 10.00pm.

CHAPTER TWENTY-ONE

A DANCE OF JESUS

DREAM, I heard and saw leaders of different nations like Churchill, Prime Minister of England, Nero of India, etc. who noticed the beauty of Uganda among all nations of the World. They envisioned Uganda's beauty in a form of jewels beautifully modeled in single beads of such amazing colours as I have never seen on the earth. The Spirit said you also have always seen the beauty of Uganda and have always given me the glory, you will wear Uganda's beautiful necklace which I am putting together myself. I saw a beautiful necklace being put together on a strand.

10th November 2010

MESSAGE, ALL ABOUT FALSE PROPHETS, EZEKIEL 13. Eventually records were found in the palace at Ecbatana in the province of Media and the King. ... And the King issued instructions not to disturb the construction of the Temple. Let it be ... He even issued a decree that those heathen pay the full construction costs without delay ... and also give priests in Jerusalem young bulls, ram and lambs for burnt offering to the God of heaven ... Anyone who attempts to change this message in any way shall have ... Ezra 6:2-11

Our God Fights our battles He is a warrior and Jehovah is His name. Exodus 15:3.

The Lord talks about rebelliousness of Israelites and we people of today. We should not harden our hearts as did the people of Israel in the wilderness; they all died there because they did not trust Him. Today if you hear God's voice speaking to you do not harden your hearts against him as the people of Israel did when they rebelled against him in the desert. Hebrews 3:15. So, if you have the potential to hold the bull by its horns in intercession, so your test is going to be to tear him up. *11th November 2010*

41ST DAY OF HONEY/WATER FAST.

Message, Reviewed the warning about the false prophets in Ezekiel 13:1-23.

Ezra sets to come to Jerusalem from Babylon. Ezra was a scribe, skilled in the law of Moses which of the Lord God of Israel had given, and the king granted him all he requested because the hand of the Lord his God was upon him. For Ezra had set his heart to study the law of the Lord and to practice it, and to become a Bible teacher, teaching those laws to the people of Israel. King Artaxerxes recognized the God of Ezra calling Him "God of Heaven" then gave a decree releasing all the people, priests and Levites to return to Jerusalem with Ezra. King Artaxerxes gave a decree to all treasurers in the provinces west of

Euphrates River to give Ezra whatever he requests of you for he is a priest and a teacher of the law of the God of heaven. ...

And whatever else the God of Heaven demands for His Temple; for why should we risk God's wrath against the king and his sons? Also, a decree of exemption of tax was given to the priests, Levites and all temple staff. The king also decreed that Ezra with the wisdom God had given him to Rule all the people of west of the Euphrates River, and teach them the laws of your God. Anyone refusing to obey the law of your God and the laws decreed of the king shall be punished immediately by death, banishment, confiscation of goods or imprisonment. ... Ezra grateful to God who demonstrated such loving kindness to him. Read on ...

When the favor of the Lord is upon you, everyone will want to serve you, even kings will make decrees in your favour; even the same enemies of the Jews who wrote a letter to the same king accusing the Jews for building the temple in Ezra 4:11.

But Jesus has far more glory than Moses, just as a man who builds a fine house gets more praise than his house does. Many people can build houses, but only God made everything. ... But Christ, God's faithful Son is in complete charge of God's house. And we Christians are God's house, He lives in us! If we keep up our courage firm, to the end, and our joy and our trust in the Lord.

And since Christ is so much ... But God was patient with them forty years, though they tried His patience sorely, He kept right on doing His mighty miracles for them to see. But God says ... for their hearts were always looking somewhere else instead of up to me, and they never found the paths I wanted them to follow. As I swore in my anger and wrath, they shall not enter my rest. ... But now is the time, Never forget the warning. "Today, if you hear God's voice speaking to you do not harden your hearts against Him as the people of Israel did when they rebelled against Him in the desert. Hebrew 3:1-15. *11th November 2010*

DREAM, A DETAILED DREAM OF KOLOLO PRINCE CHARLES Drive, the house itself burglar proof, I left there and some were bought by the occupier now, bedrooms some occupied by neighbours children, one good banana and one bad banana in the store, later were taken outside. The yard was used for stealing cars which later I saw were vandalized under cover. Strange people were coming on bikes and cars then after seeing me they turned and ran.

I was remembering all the messages God gave me while standing on the drive way of that property. Clare cleaning the garage where I was going to park my pickup, imagining how I am going to take walks on the same Hill Drive. Wondering about our path behind the boys quarters, seeing the former Mpambara's apartments still looking the same, a group of cows crossing to the neighbourhood, but one full of udder sleeps on its back to feed its calf with milk flowing. Eventually the man who had occupied my house comes and is looking uneasy as I tell him this is my house since 1980s, he was wearing false hair.

Song, "Tukutendeza Yesu" Yesu oli mwana gw'ediga.

The Lord reminded me singing that song while taking a walk on Hill Drive opposite the American Embassy. When I was about to leave I ask Him Lord, shall I ever walk these drives again? He said I will walk these drives again.

My Pledge: I am going to dance for you a dance of Jesus! I am going to dance for you a dance of the Saved!! I am going to dance for you a dance of the righteous!!!

Stepping into one of the boats, Jesus asked Simon, its owner, to push out a little into the water, so that He could sit in the boat and speak to the crowds from there: When He had finished speaking, He said to Simon, "Put out into the deep water and let down your nets for a catch." Simon answered and said 'I will do as you said and let down the nets. When they had done this, they enclosed a great quantity of fish, and their nets began to break. But when Simon Peter saw that, he fell down at Jesus' feet, saying "Go away from me Lord, for I am a sinful man." Luke 5:3-8

Our Lord cannot use you for nothing, that is what His Word says, Do not worry for what you will eat or drink or cloth, if He can cloth the flowers that even King Solomon did not have such ranges of colours those flowers and give food to the birds which do not sow or harvest. That first seek ye the kingdom of God and rest shall be added unto you!

When Jesus was preaching, also the fish came close to listen to the message of the creator. Jesus, being God and human, could see both in spirit and in physical worlds. After seeing all the fish gathered to hear His message, He asked Simon to let down the nets, John 21:4-8.

When a miracle happens some people say Go Away Lord and leave me alone I am Sinner, yet they have been toiling all the day but when things turn up, they say the fish I want, but you Lord, Go away from me. They do not want to commit themselves because they still want to enjoy the world.

They cannot spit the fish, it is sweet, and they cannot accept Jesus because He is like fire. The story of the monster that spit out the meat, he said, "no, how can I spit sweetness? And then swallow meat; he said no how can I swallow fire?" *12th November 2010*

CHAPTER TWENTY-TWO

CHULERA WEBUNDAZE

SONG, You are with me (x 3)
You are my God!!!!

DANIEL IN THE LIONS' DEN, DANIEL 6 AND 7.

Ezra was against mixed marriage when he heard the holy race had intermingled with the people of the lands, indeed that the princes and the rulers were involved in this unfaithfulness. Ezra tore his garments and pulled some of his hair and beard and sat down appalled. ... He prostrated before the Lord and said O my God, I am ashamed and embarrassed to lift up my face to you. Ezra 9:2, 6.

But beloved, we are convinced of better things concerning you, and things that accompany salvation, though we are speaking in this way, ... For God is not unjust so as to forget your work and the love which you have shown toward His name, in having ministered and in still ministering to the saints. Hebrew 6:9,10. 14th *November 2010*

45ᵀᴴ ᴅᴀʏ, As I was winding up in prayer, praying to the Spirit of the Lord to move in Tooro, after the order of Daniel 9:1 when he prayed for exiles in Babylon after 70 years, Jeremiah 27:7, and fulfilled it in 2 Chronicles 36:16. Then the Lord said to have mercy upon Israelites in exile.

Also, I was praying that may the Lord have mercy upon Tooro Kingdom and remember us, after all the abuse we have caused on the name of the Lord. The Lord asked me but you did not add Tooro on your List, He said now add on the list Tooro, Uganda, East Africa and Africa.

Message, Arise and shine, for your light has come, Isaiah 60.

Still, the issue of the mixed marriage of the holy race of God was getting serious, some leaders and elders suggested to separate from the foreign wives and their children. Ezra 10:9-11.

"You are a priest forever, after the order of Melchizedek." Hebrews 7:1-3, 17

Wait for the Results. 15ᵗʰ November 2010

Break the fast was with Kelen of Kiko who came to see me.

Dream, Defeat of the enemy; a big bull came following me closely to attack me at a close range. When I looked behind a very strong power was roughing up the bull, rolling down the hill at a very high speed, I was wondering if there would be any bones left in his body. He was mangled.

Instructions, when you pray for people, many will be healed, some will not get healed, do not wonder why, because not all will be healed for the reason only me, I know why. *16th November* 2010

Message, In 45 days of preparation many things were emptied in you and they are going to be replaced. *18th November 2010*

Song, Chulera webundaze (x 2)
Chulera webundaze, Mukama ali hanu.

Ali hanu O wamananu
   Ali hanu Omuliisa
   Ali hanu Owembabazi
   Ali hanu akulindirire

Ali hanu kukukiza!!
   Ali hanu kukucwamu

Lirirra Omwoyo gwawe
   Mukama arakuganyira
   Mugambire ebikulemere
   Mugambire Yesu!!

Ija iwe nkoku ali

Emikono ohanikire
Uwe wenka arakutangirra
Gwa habigere bye!!!

Yesu wembabazi mali
Tabinga muntu weena
Bona bona abagaanyira
Naiwe arakutangirra
20th November 2010

CHAPTER TWENTY-THREE

PRAYER FOR TOORO KINGDOM

AMOS 3:3-7

I dreamed a beautiful design made on my right thigh at first looked like small veins, which later formed into an inner design like an internal tattoo. I was sitting on a stool being prepared like a most beautiful bride for four years. For Persecution of Christians I prayed a special prayer to cover Christians to be obscured against their executors. I was having two offices with one in Kyarusozi Tea Estates and another one in Kampala, and having two radios a big one and another one small but powerful.

At evening as I was praying when I heard in the spirit that the men are bringing your plane (Abasaija baliyo nibaleta enyonyi yawe). 22nd November 2010

ABOUT THE LOVE OF GOD, sow to yourselves in righteousness, reap in mercy; break up your fallow ground: for it is time to seek the Lord, till he come and rain righteousness upon you. Ye have plowed wickedness, ye have reaped iniquity; ye have eaten the fruit of lies: because thou didst trust in thy way, in the multitude of thy mighty men. Hosea 10:12-13.

I was so consumed with the Love of God I left the office at 3.00pm, came home and was so tensed up with the Love of God. To love God is something which cannot be valued with anything on the planet earth, it is valueless, it is beyond any riches, or wealth of the universe. It is eternity itself.

The love of God is to be cultivated with time, you cannot buy it, you cannot bribe to get it. It cannot be pumped into a person. You work it out with time, you build it like a wall by putting a brick on a brick. It grows gradually and steadily, it does not work with high, panic, or competition (katiko, kapapo, kalitango, kajabirro). It works with patience, trust, faith, consistence, denying self, spending time to listen and letting Him know your heart. *23rd November 2010*

"ASK WHAT YOU WANT." CONTINUED FROM 7TH OCTOBER QUESTION

On 15th November 2010 on the 45th day I was in the village. As I was winding up in prayer, praying to the Spirit of the Lord to move in Tooro. After the order of Daniel when he prayed for exiles in Babylon after 70 years as Jeremiah had predicted in Jeremiah 27:7, as it was fulfilled in 2 Chronicles 36:16. Then the Lord said to have mercy upon Israelites in exile later in Daniel 9:1, Ezra and Nehemiah.

Also, I was praying that may the Lord have mercy upon Tooro Kingdom and remember us, after all the abuse, we have called on the name of the Lord. The Lord asked me. "But you did not add Tooro on your List?" He said now add on the list Tooro, Uganda, East Africa and Africa."

Prayer for Tooro, Lord, Tooro, in the 1920s is the Kingdom which was next to become elite after Buganda Kingdom; Tooro king Kamurasi and Bishop Balya interpreted the Bible, the 3rd Bible in Rutooro after the Luganda and Swahili Bibles. King Kamurasi's heart was after the Lord, he gave orders to wipe out all witchcraft in Tooro. He abolished idolatry and gave up all his concubines and remained with one wife who was my great, great aunt.

He did good in your site and Tooro prospered, they were the ones to be educated, they sent teachers, doctors, court assessors, administrators in all Ankole, Kigezi, which is now Kabale, Bunyoro, Kasese, Bundibugyo and up to the boarders of Congo where my father was a Chief from 1946-1949.

From 1936 king George Rukidi's reign, he did not follow in his father's steps, witchcraft returned in the kingdom, he restored idolatry got himself many wives and did abominations of incest. From 1960s Tooro's name and fame in the whole of Uganda became an abuse, the language they used to admire, it sounded like French, and it sounded musical, became a dingy for use in music dance and drama. The Batooro women who were sort everywhere to become wives of kings and chiefs of other kingdoms because of their education, good culture and neatness became prostitutes.

Tooro was rich with cattle, they were all vaccinated and all died in a matter of weeks, because they refused to go and cultivate in the British Estates. Therefore Batooro became lazy and resorted to drinking because they were cattle keepers who were not used to hard labour. When the old folks expired the remnants escaped to the big city where they could make ends meet and became collectors of bottles and cans, wheel-barrow pushers with all kinds of odd jobs for survival.

Prayer, Now, Lord of Heaven and Earth, I pray forgive

Tooro race: - for misuse of our language, instead of Worshiping You.

- for laziness,
- for prostitution,
- for witchcraft,
- for idolatry,
- for jealousy,
- for envy,
- for hatred,
- for murder,
- drunkenness,
- for disobedience to your counsel,
- for pride,
- for too much self-esteem,
- for hating you,
- for incest,
- for rape and defilement,
- for animosity,
- for homosexuality,
- for gay,
- for lesbianism,
- for rebellion against You,
- for abortions,
- for adultery,
- for foul language,
- for esteeming ancestor heritage,
- for esteeming clan heritage,
- for religious spirits,
- for theft,
- for sex with animals,
- for believing in water spirits,
- for believing in underworld spirits,

- for believing in heavenly hosts of the sun, moon and stars,
- for suicide spirits,
- for cannibalism,
- for embracing the false doctrine of Bisaka,
- for child molestation,
- for child sacrifice,
- for blaspheming your Spirit,
- for night dancing,
- for breaking all your Ten Commandments.

Lord! Uproot, tear, pry, disentangle all the evil tentacles mentioned above, which bind Tooro into slavery and make Tooro prisoners to the devil.

Lord, have mercy on us, I stand in the gap of Tooro, I am in the line of king Kamurasi, by spirit and blood, who had a heart for you, and now I stand to plead for Tooro because suffering for over 70 years, have Mercy upon us, O! Lord, and remember the fear of God and sin which was in our king Kamurasi and the Love to do Your Will. Lord, restore and wash Tooro with Your precious blood from boundaries: In the east from Mubende, in the west from Congo Republic, in the north from Bunyoro Kingdom, and in the South from Ankole Kingdom.

Lord, one day You asked "Whom can I send?" in Isaiah 6:8, Lord, I also say "Here I am, send me to Tooro Kingdom; though the boundaries are no longer observed but You know where they are, also send me to Uganda, East Africa and other places in Africa Continent. Let the people of Tooro return to You, let them remember where they erred and repent.

Therefore, Lord, as Tooro caused Your name to be abused, blasphemed, laughed at and they swore Your name in vain, which angered You, like the Israelites, You scattered Batooro in all nations never to come back home and build homes and businesses in the land You gave to us.

After forgiving us, Lord! May You use Your maid servant or servant You choose to empty hell and fill Heaven with souls of every language, colour and nations of the world. The people You created right from the beginning of the world which the enemy took by deception. For the soul of man to You is more than all the valuable treasures created in heaven above, on earth, under the earth, on water, or underwater; all put together cannot purchase a soul of man for a second.

Lord! Let there be in Tooro, Uganda, East Africa, Africa a treasure pool which will draw souls from continents of Africa, Europe, Asia, North America, South America, Australia and Antarctica to come to seek after the treasure of salvation and healing of the nations. Let people spread maps in front of them to locate where Tooro is.

Let the Batooro also stand with their heads up and say "God has answered us not with perishable treasures but has blessed us with eternity treasures." Amen. 24th November 2010

CHAPTER TWENTY-FOUR

BE FAITHFUL TO BE FILLED, BA MWESIGWA

I AM EMPTYING you of dust, and steady filling you with gold, emptying stones in steady filling you with diamonds.

Expression, "This mountain of life" means that life is like a mountain we are taking one step at a time. One day at a time. 25th *November 2010*

IN THE WORLD, A PRISONER IF HE IS CONDEMNED FOR 25 years when he works well his days are reduced, so they are counted down instead of serving 25 years they count day and night and you serves 12 and half years. But in spiritual realm the counting is doubled, when you go through trials and situations for the sake of the kingdom, days are doubled if you go through 25 years, it counts 50 years of reward. 26th *November 2010*

Message. Blow ye the trumpet in Zion, and sound an alarm in my holy mountain: let all the inhabitants of the land tremble: for the day of the Lord cometh, for it is nigh at hand; Joel 2. All. *27th - 30th November 2010*

Make a large signpost and write on it the birth announcement of the son I am going to give you. – Use capital letters! His name will be Maher - shalal - hash - baz, which means "Your Enemies will soon be destroyed." ... Do not fear anything except the Lord of the armies of heaven! If you fear Him, you need not fear nothing else. ... I will wait for the Lord to help us, though He is hiding Now! My only hope is in Him. I and the children God has given me have symbolic names that reveal the plans of the Lord of Heaven's armies for his people," Isaiah 8, All.

The Lord had given me this scripture before on 14th November 2007. After the Spirit of the Lord gave me Isaiah's family names also, I wrote down my family names:

Isaiah = "Jehova will save His people"

Shear- jashub = "A remnant shall return"

Maher – shalal – hash – baz = "Your enemies will soon be destroyed." *1st December 2010*

Early in the morning after prayers, in vision a blank cheque. And was asked if you are asked to fill in the figure how much can you put there?

Answer: First and foremost, I have to list the tasks I would like to accomplish and justify them before I fill in the figures in the cheque.

- Nakumatt for Christians Plot
- Construction of the Plot
- Furnishing
- Nyamabuga Foundation Schools
- NNS/NPS Complex
- Multipurpose
- NSS Complex
- NSS Boarding and other facilities
- NHS
- NCU
- Nyamabuga Spiritual Development
- Vocational Bible School
- Pastors and Church Leaders' Centre
- Evangelization
- Youth Group Complex
- Skills Development Projects
- Girl Child Development Projects Complex
- Nyamabuga Women's Entrepreneurs

Lord please may you add on my name "Hakire Kabatalemwa," (At least Kabatalemwa). 2nd *December* 2010

WARNING ABOUT FALSE IDOL WORSHIP, EZEKIEL 8.

In Nigeria if caught in drug trafficking one has to spend 27 years in prison or pay fine of 1 million Nairas. In Nigeria a Judge was put on a task when the court brokers brought a file of his daughter who was caught in drug trafficking. So, when the Judge took his seat, in front of him there was his daughter. The Judge did not show any concern and judged her as he would have judged anybody and passed the file to the court brokers, and dismissed the proceedings until 2.00pm o'clock.

As soon as he left the courtroom he entered his chambers and removed the judge's gowns, he dashed across the street to the bank and withdrew 1 million Nairas, went to the accounts department and paid the fine of his daughter. The court officials were concerned why did he pay the fine for his daughter and not let her go and serve the sentence. He answered them accordingly that what the court needed was either pay the fine or the girl go to prison, now he had paid the fine and his daughter needed not to go to prison!!!

Our heavenly father is more than that judge, for Him He had to send His real son to come and pay our ransom. You cannot go to prison now for all what you have done because He paid it all.

9th December 2010

Dreamt, about a big tree with no leaves but full of bird's nests weaved nearly on every branch.

Vision, two brand new steel safes one big another one small on a truck. The Holy Spirit said those are your safes.

Wondering to myself that on a certain occasion the Lord is going to prepare for me, I have few relatives left to invite.

In the bathroom the Lord spoke to me that "Many will long to be invited, even your enemies, but will not have that opportunity." I have placed you in a High and Respected position." Therefore, I will reveal my name to my people and they shall know the power in that Name. Then at last they will recognize that it is I, Yes, I who speaks to them. Salvation and crucifixion prophesies, Isaiah 52, All important. 12th December 2010

IF YE WILL NOT BELIEVE, SURELY YE SHALL NOT BE established. Isaiah 7:1-9.

Message, Be faithful to be filled, (Ba Mwesigwa).

15th December 2010

MESSAGE, BE FAITHFUL (OBE MWESIGWA). I SAID LORD, I cannot promise except I will pray for it every time, as I pray for my Salvation. Because the Word says My salvation is not of yesterday but of today.

Taking a siesta in the office, I saw a ring of black diamond and its facets and I asked the Lord are there black Diamonds? Then I saw yellow diamond and was asked what is the name of that; I said Topaz. Then a green one and was asked its name also, I said Emerald, then the name turquoise of another precious stone. I heard one time I spoke to you about the liquid diamond or gold.

People say I do not play drummer "what about getting one from being a gate keeper and making him a prime minister, or making a slave a jailbird into a prime minister of Egypt. Is that not drummer who can believe that? **Message**, Isaiah 7:3, 4, 11 and 14. 15th December 2010

CHAPTER TWENTY-FIVE

I AM PLAN B

MESSAGE, Prophesy of Christ's coming, Isaiah 9.

Prayer, Lord, in 1982 you told me that "I will never forget the tears you have cried for me." Therefore, may the angels put in place silos of the tears I cry, Silo of salvation prayers and a silo of every prayer of faithfulness I pray every *t*ime. My heart was rejoicing in the Lord my God.

Spiritual Heavenly colours and their meanings:

- Gold - Deity
- Silver - Redemption
- Brass - Suffering
- Blue - Son of God
- Purple - Jesus the King
- Red - Saviour
- Goats hair - Prophet
- White - Purity perfect
- Ram - substitute
- Burge skin – Jesus suffering on a cross
- Satin Wood - Incorruptible

- Oil - Anointed the Love of God for His Faithful People

16th December 2010

GOD IS JEALOUS OVER THOSE HE LOVES, THAT IS WHY HE takes vengeance on those who hurt them. He furiously destroys their enemies. Nahum 1:2

God is so faithful He does not forget His faithful servants: They sent soldiers to bring Jeremiah out of the prison and put him into the care of Gedaliah to take him back to his home. The Lord gave a Word to Jeremiah for Ebedmelech the Ethiopian when he was still in prison that "The Lord of Hosts the God of Israel says; I will do this city everything I threatened; I will destroy it before your eyes, but I will deliver you, you shall not be killed by those you fear so much. As a reward for trusting me I will preserve your life and keep you safe." Jeremiah 39, 40.

Also the Lord sent Jeremiah to tell Baruch "O! Baruch, the Lord God of Israel says this to you "You have said, Woe is me ... Jeremiah 45:3-5. 17th December 2010

WORD OF KNOWLEDGE: PASTOR D NKATA SENT ME A message that I go to attend a business fellowship of a preacher from Tanzania who makes $100,000 per month. In my heart I decided that I will not go there for the reason; the Lord told Rick Joyner in his book 'The Call' that "If you put together all the treasures or riches from the whole world they cannot purchase a man's soul for one second."

This tells me I am so, so wealthy, more than any person can imagine. Also, when I consider the Scripture in Eccl. 3:11 that says that "He created eternity in the hearts of men, even so, man cannot see the beginning to the end." Man does not know his value, when we come to the Lord, we need to know who we are. The Word says Seek ye first the kingdom of God and the rest will be added to you."

18th December 2010

As I was meditating on "Ba Mwesigwa" message of 15TH December 2010 above, this message crashed me. I prayed 'Lord, to be faithful, takes one a daily prayer, as salvation, wisdom, obedience, humility, etc. this is a situation, a crisis or a challenge which changes with time for example Solomon met that situation of the two prostitute once in his life, the queen of Sheba visited him once and he had to give judgment, counsel according to the situation as it presented itself.

Also, Daniel one day judged Suzan's case where she was going to be executed on falsehood of the church elders, but the Lord gave Daniel wisdom at that moment for that situation.

Therefore, Lord whenever there is need for faithfulness, wisdom, obedience or humility let it be given for that situation at that very moment. As in the book of Corrie Ten Boom she says that "When she was young, she told her dad that she was not scared to be a Christian, but what she feared most was to die as a martyr for Jesus Christ." Her dad told her that when the time comes, she will receive the grace for it. He told her that a train ticket is not purchase in a week's advance. That you purchase a ticket when you are going to board therefore, when the time comes for you to die as a martyr will get the grace.

Prayer, Lord, whenever I need to be faithful, when I need wisdom, obedience, humility and salvation let me bring it to you as the situation or challenge presents itself give me the Grace. Amen.

Message, Judgment for idolatry, Jeremiah 44:16-18.

19th December 2010, after midnight

EACH PERSON IS AN INDIVIDUAL, HE IS ON HIS OWN SETUP NO matter what similarities one has with one another. The Lord spoke to my heart that even identical twins are never the same from the very minute they are born, there is a time difference, and that makes them different. Identical twins do not do things at the very same time; they have different times of doing things, though they may have the same choice of colour but it may be a different design, style or fashion. They think differently, their thoughts are not the same. Therefore, each person is an individual in this world and God has a different calling on each one's life. *27th December 2010*

I AM TURNING ALL MY RICHES TO YOU!!! BE TRUST-WORTH, be faithful, gather my people, tell my people all colours, all languages and all nations. *29th December 2010*

IT IS NOT ONLY BAPTISM, BUT THE WASHING AWAY YOUR SINS is by confession, Acts 22:16

Message, But what saith it? The word is nigh thee, even in thy mouth, and in thy heart: that is, the word of faith, which we preach; That if thou shalt confess with thy mouth the Lord Jesus, and shalt believe in thine heart that God hath raised him from the dead, thou shalt be saved. Romans 10:8-9.

Religious spirit, people can even Fight kill for the sake of religion, leaving Christ outside, moreover that show they killed Him the King of Glory, thinking that they were right, Jesus was wrong. Saul (Paul) though he was more godly to the extent of killing/executing Christians (the saved) who were walking with Christ, until he recognized Jesus Christ, confessed and got born again. Jesus started using him among gentiles. Acts 22:20. *30th December 2010*

I AM PLAN B FOR THE SALVATION PLAN. OUR LORD CAME down from heaven on Plan A to save people, when the enemy had stolen the keys from Adam. When our Lord returned to heaven the enemy again deceived people even those who had known the truth, he followed them in the churches and bound them there with religion, witchcraft, idolatry, satanism, etc.

Before I went to pray I decided to lie down first. In a vision I saw "the Lion of Judah's Crown of thorns on His head and the pierced palms and the keys as on the painting at All Nations. *31st December 2010*

MY PLEDGE TO THE LORD IS PLAN B TO WORK OUT MY salvation with fear and trembling. Pray for the true salvation, obedience, wisdom, faithfulness and humility as often as possible as situations and challenges come in different styles and fashions daily. *1st January 2011*

DREAM, EARLY IN THE MORNING, I WAS STANDING UNDER A big tree with a doctor, when I saw a big snake looking at me. I called people to see it, it turned to go and looked so big no one could kill it with a stick. As I was wondering how to kill it, I found myself at Diamond Trust Building and all town people had gathered looking at it. Some on top of the wall. As I was watching, that snake rolled itself in a big ball like a tire and flew over heads and threw itself in another building over Total Petrol Station. Now it looked as if it was rolled in mud or dust it looked so brown, as I was wondering I found myself again standing in a yard and it came flying in a form of an ambulance light bulb and stood in front of me. I found myself having a good sized stick to kill it, I started removing the obstacles on the way to smash it. It was there watching me.

I woke up disappointed, but in the spirit I heard that it was not possible to kill it with the stick, I was reminded the 1980s trick the Lord gave me to use hot water, but this time it has to be plenty of it in a big container to reach it using a horse to flash that snake.

I forced myself to sleep thinking that the Lord would bring me a solution to kill that snake. At 7.00am Clare called me on Allan's phone excited, telling me of a battle warned. She was telling me a similar dream of a big snake in a tree that no one could manage to kill it, unless one had a gun, that she started to look for a policeman with a gun but Gonzaga came with a person with an old gun and the snake was killed and started falling from the tree roll by roll. That the snake looked purple and it looked as if it had not died completely and it was looking at me and I was so close to confirm its death; Clare kept screaming at me that the snake could jump at me until it completely died.

So, the dream of Clare was a continuation of mine that the snake was at long last killed.

Praise the Lord!!! 2nd *January 2011*

Prayer: Lord save me from the spirit of compromise as each individual has his and her own calling and challenges. Also save me from the spirit of copying, let me always do my own as the Spirit leads me. I pray for the spirit of clarity and fluent in my speech, not as Larry King of CNN, but in a way, you want me to communicate to your people.

Lying on my bed in a vision I saw live bricks building spiritual walls into a house, when I sleep my spiritual house will be built with live bricks, full of live praise, prayer, exaltation and adoration. 5th *January 2011*

MICAH 7 YOU HAVE DECIDED TO GIVE ME THE 1ST PLACE IN your life, I will also give you the 1st place in My Heart. You have decided to Fight my enemy, I will Fight your enemies too.

A friend said that she will never cry for money, you did not turn or take it for yourself for gains. 25.5m instead of making it money you opted for the souls for the kingdom of God.

I shared the dream of a huge snake, instead of using it crushing your enemies, you took it to be the enemy of the nation which had come to swallow it, in a form of homo and gay. 6th *January 2011*

CHAPTER TWENTY-SIX

WISDOM SPOKE

EARLY IN THE morning Wisdom came and told me you have too much in your hands which may cause you a breakdown or stress.

- You are intending to travel - ticket
- You are constructing a school - money is needed
- You are still paying for the van hire purchase
- You are to pay half of Kabaganda's land at Nyamabuga
- You are to finish up Maguli's money
- You are to pay DHL
- You are putting up the Nursery School

Now if you look for a new house to go to, they will require you to pay upfront 3 months.

Houses are in dollars, here. They want two months pay which is 1.4m/=. Why don't you stay and pay that up to March? In February you leave for US, by the time you return the Lord would have given you a direction.

Wisdom spoke to my heart before I left for work and said do not force yourself in the thoughts of people unless it is out of the line of the counsel of the Holy Spirit. You will take nothing out of this house to the next house I am giving you. This house you are living in, compared with the one I am giving you, this one is like a rug. I am going to give you a furnished house where you will lack nothing. *11th January 2011*

GOD HAS A PURPOSE FOR YOU FROM THE TIME OF CREATION, When God has a purpose for your life He separates you, from clans, ancestors, relationships, friends in order to completely depend on Him. Relationships screen us from the purpose of God. Human beings are dependents, they always look for the shoulder to cry on whenever there is a situation. But when the Lord wants to fulfill His purpose in you He removes all the crying shoulders, so that you can cry on His Shoulder only and know that He is God.

The Lord told Abraham Go forth from your country and from your relatives and from your father's house, to the land which I will show you and I will make you a great Nation. Genesis 12:1-2 Promise/Purpose. Abraham left nephew Lot, when God has a purpose for you, He asks you to take the journey alone.

Human beings like company, we always feel we have to have somebody with us. Which often results into a stumbling blocks on our way, e.g. one day the Lord showed me some family whose child had taken poison and He wanted me to go and pray for them, but I went with the Pastor, the Lord had asked me to pray for them but I feared to pray for them when the pastor was standing there and I asked him to pray, the results when I went back home were not good.

However, Abraham carried his nephew Lot Now Lot who

went with Abram also had flocks and herds and tents. And the land could not sustain them while dwelling together. God sent away Lot in peace, in order to fulfill the calling of Abraham. He wanted to remain with Abraham. The Lord said to Abram after Lot had separated from him; Now lift up your eyes and look from the place where you are, northward and southward and eastward and westward; for all the land which you see I will give to you and to your descendants forever. Arise, walk about the land through its length and breadth; for I will give it to you. Gen. 12, 13.

Message, Abram promised a son. Behold the Word of the Lord came to him saying; This man will not be your heir; but one who will come forth, from your own body, he shall be your heir. The promise was between Abram and God. I am God Almighty walk before Me, and be blameless. I will establish my covenant between me and you I will multiply you exceedingly. Gen. 15-17.

God purposed Abraham to inheritance Canaan land for an everlasting possession for the Israelites and covenanted with Abraham, because He knew that Jesus was going to come through that race. Gen 17:7-8.

When God has "Purposed you," He shares with you His heart, The Lord said, "Shall I hide from Abraham what I am about to do" Since He Purposed Abraham to be a Father of Faith, He talked to him alone; he said, Abraham take now your son, your only son whom you love, Isaac, and go to the land of Moriah, and offer him on one of the mountain I will show you. Gen. 18-22.

Each one of us God has called us individually. Ask the Lord's PURPOSE for your life. When Abraham was left alone the Lord came and promised him Isaac. A child of Faith which caused Abraham to be called a "Father of Faith."

The Lord called Abraham alone, He had a plan a purpose for

his life Heart to Heart teaching. The Lord created everybody with a purposed life for His Kingdom but people walk out of His purpose and go to do their own. We are called to do the Lord's Will on earth, but the world sacks out the Godly purpose and replace it with its Own vanity. Many people's famishes caused them to block the purpose God created them to fulfill because they say what will my family think of me if I get saved? I was born in Catholic, protestant, or Muslim family. What will they think of me to join? Christians who are considered mad, fanatics, etc. because religion has made them to lose the calling of God for the purpose God called them to fulfill; due to fear of what the clergy, sheik, nun, or brother thinks of me. But when the Lord calls you, He calls you alone. Your tongue, your uncontrolled tongue, can stand in the way to not fulfill the purpose of God. Your looks can deceive you and find yourself losing your purposed life God prepared for you. You think that your looks can buy you friends and all what you need, yet it can leave you or can be ruined e.g. old age, acid cases, accident, etc. Your untamed eyes can force you to go to places where you should not have gone, e.g. football and the World Cup horror in 2011, car races, or movies; many people have perished just because they wanted to go to feed the eyes.

Human wisdom has caused many people delusions and deceived many out of the Purpose when thinking that they know, yet they do not know the ways of the Lord. Who can tell how miracles happen. Pride is what has made many men and women of God to lose their purpose, it is the most effective tool the enemy uses to destroy the servants of God.

Familiarization causes servants of God to be deceived into thinking that they know the Lord, very much to the extent of calling and singing songs and equating Him with human names like Mzee, my boyfriend, my Old man. Familiarization in disrespect of His Word in bad jokes and making fun of the Word. *12th January 2011*

CHAPTER TWENTY-SEVEN

GENUINE DOORS AND A FALSE DOOR

ESTHER 1 AND 2.

Prayer, O! Lord, Let not my human wisdom be a barrier to do your purpose. Let my pride not stand and shield me to your purpose I am called to fulfill. Lord help me not to fall in the sin of familiarization to your Word and You. Lord you created my life; sheave, strain, shift, and winnow out the old life and give me your new life to do the purpose you called for me. I have been liberated from wrong thoughts, vile speech and walk. I have been liberated from clans, ancestor, relationships and friendship attachments which entangle me. I have been redeemed from the ancestral, great grand, grandparents, both paternal, maternal, and self-involved DNA which kept collecting on me along the way from the time when our grandparents sinned in the Garden to the time of my conception to date. I return to my origin of creation Holy and Pure as the Creator intended my DNA. Amen. 13th January 2011

Prayer, Lord, help me to mark what I see in my vision, and what I hear in the Spirit of my destination. Help me to look for the path and means to reach WHERE You have called me to righteousness. Help me to make a Map of daily walk for thoughts in words.

Help me to avoid doors which are attractively opened, but not by You. Help me to hear and obey, to do what Your still small Voice instructs me to do. And lead me to see doors which are opened by You. Amen.

Prayer, Lord, help me to do away with my false humility. Use me for what You desire me to do. Let me not look to my inadequacy but to Your adequacy. Let me not complain how inadequate, unworthy, and incompetent I am; but look at You and what You are going to accomplish in me. Amen. 20th *January 2011*

I met an Ambassador who took me to his office and gave me a registration form for the Great East African Oil Conference to take place from 2nd – 4th February 2011. He encouraged me to register and attend for the sake of meeting big people from all over the world. He mentioned to me that "The Mbiires and Karuhangas would not be where they are, if they did not crash on such gatherings." You never know whom you meet there, just harness yourself to another company and make a joint venture in order to use this conference. He said the oil exploration in Uganda in 2020 is going to be a big wave of wealthy investors in East Africa.

Back at home I sat with Clare and shared that "some people in high circles now have minds framed "Oil" as everything within an end itself." I said suppose now God who created oil and other minerals says "let the oil stop there," what would those who are putting all their hopes in oil do? The first explored oil was in Rwebisengo - Butuku and all the equipment to drill it were put in place, but something wrong happened, all the equipments are still there standing. Many people had gone to get plots but all stopped there. "Fear God and Respect Him!!!"

21st January 2011

ON THE INTERNET I SAW A MAN HOLDING A CHUNK OF GOLD that it was weighing 10 kgs, and I read that this is the biggest chunk of gold ever found. I objected, because the Lord told me in 1998, that His is the only one who knows where he stored the biggest chunk of gold and can give it to whom who pleases Him.

Prayer, Lord, you said on 21st September 2006 and the witness inside me, "Sleep until that sleep is finished out of you, do not be like religious people,."On this cement where you have continued sleeping you think will not be rewarded, everything you do for the sake of the kingdom, however small, it cannot go without being rewarded." Lord, always no one knows or tells the promised reward until he or she receives it. Now I pray Lord, may I in that reward receive positive results in prayer for the Kingdom and against the powers of darkness. Amen.

Message, slept and woke up at 2.00a.m and got this: Opening Genuine Doors and a False Door. There are easy and attractive Doors one can easily open and it is always tempting to look for such doors but they are not always the ones we need to help us fulfill our destiny. Do not choose doors by their appearance, but always ask the Holy Spirit to help you. The Holy Spirit in his own way creates or looks for his own ways and means or shortcuts to make things happen; but man with the

Spirit of God looks to God to make things happen. *22nd January 2011*

EARLY IN THE MORNING I HEARD TWO ORIGINAL COPIES. I prayed and cancelled it and then came the original. I saw on white, gloss, beautiful folder a hand opened it; before I could see what was inside it closed. We had a party for the P7 leavers who passed their examination. *26th January 2011*

ON THE WAY GOING BACK TO KAMPALA FROM THE VILLAGE. As usual in my spirit I started talking to the Lord about what He told me or Nakumatt for Christians, I said Lord, I would not mind about Nakumatt, but my worry is when are you returning? In my spirit I heard to come I will come, but if I come who is ready? Many will be left and you also may not make it. I stopped to think and said, true Lord. This I have always seen myself, my thoughts, words and actions betray me, that is why I keep repenting telling you I cannot make it on my own except by your grace. My righteousness is filthy rags, but as the Bible says in Revelations that some will have to go through fire. I do not mind if you make it possible for me to go through fire but may I reach heaven. *27th January 2011*

DREAM, I WAS AT THE ROAD JUNCTION GOING HOME, TWO lions appeared a male and a female, but I was controlling them with such ease by talking to them in a love language. They would come to me and I pat them like dogs but people were so scared and I told the people to keep their voices low so that the Lions would not be aroused and attack them. Meanwhile I was wondering when Bro Roland will be coming. Then Bro Roland came in a big a beautiful coaster driving at a high speed and my heart rested that at least he has come; he will relieve me of the control of the lions. 30th *January 2011*

CHAPTER TWENTY-EIGHT

DO NOT CHOOSE DOORS BY THEIR APPEARANCE

OPENING genuine doors and false doors, there are easy attractive doors one can easily open, and it is always tempting to look for such doors, but they are not always the ones we need to help us fulfill our destiny. Do not choose doors by their appearance, but always ask the Holy Spirit to help you.

When I first went to the US in January 1989 to attend a Morris Cerullo World Conference the Lord opened the door for me through a 78 years old lady called Sis Agnes Numer. It took twenty-one years before I realized the fruits of that open door.

Do not choose doors by their appearance, but always ask the Holy Spirit to help you. The Holy Spirit creates or looks for his own ways and means or short cuts to make things happen; but man with the Spirit of God looks to God to make things happen. He does not push, e.g. when I was in Baton Rouge ministering in a home, one person asked me whether I needed a truck, as I was trying to explain one suggested two tractors and the discussion went on back and forth, by the end of the meeting the decision had been passed without me taking part in it. 22nd *January 2011*

MESSAGE, YOU WERE PURPOSED AND DESTINED. EPHESIANS 1:3-14. Purposed Life, You are an Island.

I was on the way to the village to preach at Kyarusozi Fellowship. On the way I saw so many areas were burnt, as usual, as it is a norm for the month of January and February, people burn old grass so that new grass would grow for animals. This time I realized near the road and further, that there were islands of unburnt grass, though the fire came close and burnt all the grass around but that island of green grass but this island was left intact. This looks like the islands which are surrounded by water all the land is submerged by water, but the invisible protecting hands of the almighty which says so far and no further to the fire and water.

Why were you not born dead? Why did you not die of diseases which attacked you?

You were at one time or another hospitalized and there was no hope that you were going to make it but you survived accidents where other people died, etc. Why? The Lord has a call on your life!! e hHeHe has a purpose for your life which He is going to fulfill. Dan. 11:32b.

That is why He has made you an "Island" fire has consumed everyone around you and has protected you, and you remained standing alone with your husband, alone with your wife, alone with your children, alone with your mother, alone with your dad, alone without friends.

There are many types of fires now consuming your neighbours with water submerging around about. There is rebellion, the fire and water in the youths whether in church or secular world doing drugs, gangs, murder, alcohol, fornication, piercing spirit, tattooing spirit, obscene music abusing God like Rap, gays and abortions rights, idolatry, cults, doctrines, satan worship, covenants, agreements and contracts with satan, etc., e.g. ritual murder at Washington Airport an appeal: Who killed a little girl?

There are fires, waters, tornados, tsunamis, and diseases consuming the next bush: cancer, diabetes, heart attacks in developed countries, wars, AIDS and poverty in Africa. There are fires of calamities and disasters consuming the neighbourhoods; e.g. 2010 Haiti and Chile earthquakes, Bududa landslide, Kasubi tombs fire in Uganda, 2011 Japan earthquake and tsunami, 100 tornados, Patomic River flood in Maryland and Mississippi overflowing the banks and leaving so many homeless as unheard of for centuries.

You have been called and purposed to take your stand as an island to do the Will of God at a rebellious hour when people in authority are protecting the abusers, rapists, defilers, gays, homosexuals while persecuting those who stand to Fight the evil doers.

The Church of God is mixed up, people's ears are itching to hear only lies of the enemy. They do not hear the rebukes of the Lord. The evil is good and the good is evil. The enemy has entered the Church and made it a Social Club where people go to socialize. They calculate time for the Lord, here we do things like ... False shepherds are tearing the sheep, over milking the sheep, collecting homeless, orphan kids on the street and sodomizing them in the church without the fear of God.

Righteousness is measured by success, i.e. a Pastor called me to go and hear a preacher from Tanzania that he wanted to tell us how to make $100,000 per week.

There is the shaking of nations, leaders, churches and their pastors. Only the island God has left standing in the midst of burnt acres or in the midst of water is going to stand the shaking on 3 pillars: the Word, Prayer and Fellowship. Nahum 1:3.

At the end of the journey a sister saw a thin tight string across the valley where you, yourself, will be required to walk across, the requirement is: you will have to be light as a feather with righteousness and obedience, know when to Camp, when to March and when to Fight. *6th February 2011*

CHAPTER TWENTY-NINE

DECEPTION OF THE ENEMY

IN THE USA.
9th February - 27th April 2011

THE DECEPTION OF THE ENEMY, THE LORD TOLD ME ABOUT the deception of the enemy how he deceives people into believing his lies to accept diseases he throws to them. It starts as a pricking pin, one accepts it, it becomes more harder and painful as one accepts, then becomes a lump then he or she goes to see a doctor who diagnoses it and gives it a name. Now, one is thrown in fear and starts telling people how he or she has been diagnosed with cancer, diabetes, etc. *11th February 2011*

WHEN I WAS IN THE BATHROOM I LAUGHED SO MUCH WHEN I asked myself "the satanists are anxiously waiting for Nimrod to come and finish the Tower of Babylon: What about the one who stopped it and dispersed them, is He not still the same person, satan is a liar."

LEANING INTO THE WIND, by A. W. TOZER, THE REVIVAL breeze is strongly blowing and scarcely no one appears to have the discernment or the courage to turn around and "Lean into the Wind." Religion has its vogue much as do philosophies of politics and women's fashions found in Girl Power Magazine. Historically the major, stream line, world religions have their periods of decline and recovery which are bluntly called Revivals by Thea nihilistic cult of Moslems, Catholics as well as Protestants are having revivals to describe the phenomenon, without calling on the elevation or change of the moral standards of its devotees.

These religions with popular Christianity, could enjoy a boom together living without and divorced from the transforming power of the Holy Spirit and so leave the Church of Christ of the next generation in worse situation than it would have been if the boom had never occurred.

We do not need revival but a radical reformation that will go to the root of our moral and spiritual diseases and maladies to deal with causes rather than symptoms).

Tozer's opinion is that under the present circumstance we do not want revival at all. A wide spread revival of the kind of Christianity of today might prove or bring a moral tragedy from which we would not recover in 100 years.

My opinion is people are playing church with no serious transformation of heart. Church is in the world and the world is in the church. Young gospel singers are copying every kind of behaviour of secular singers of rock, hip hop and rap stars and they try to be so much like them with their mannerism of shooting "V" finger sign.

What is rap? They do not know it is acting in backward movements, backward writing of satan-natas, e.g. God-Dog, which was invented by a satanist man called Aliester Crowley, the author of Black Magic which he created to supersede Christianity. His mother called him the Beast. He is the one who started to use 666 and his book, called 777 of Quablistic teaching and writing to get power in music, actors, singers, etc. (Tru-Church info).

Crowley Alliester Magic Tips says: Let him train himself to think backwards by external means as set let him train himself: to learn to write backward, learn to walk backward, listen to phonograph records reversed, practice speaking backwards, learn to read backwards, and instead of saying "I am he" let him say "eh ma I" satan is natas.

Church leaders cannot differentiate dress code for the Church and the street, women are painting themselves. Dark shadows in women singers, pastors' wives, women leaders in the church, etc. Marilyn Manson is now the head of the Church of the Free Mansions, she paints her face white to represent death and also darkens her eyes with heavy black eye shadows as satanic, but the ladies in the Christian churches think it's modern.

The Pastors invite any person who says "Praise the Lord." Pastors now lie, steal, do witchcraft, even are homosexuals and gay pastors.

The Beatles – used Crowley principles when they called him Sgt. Pepper Adam. They have started a "Rock Band Gang" to attract the youth.

Alliester Crowley, 666, The Beast, is in high governments of the world. On the $1 bill there is the unfinished tower and eye there. Some government heads are Free Mansions, e.g. UK. They say "He" approves all our undertakings; who?

There is an Organization of 300 Alumni they know what you do not know. ORDO Templi Orientis Organization OTO – fraternal order their law is of Crowley the Beast: "Do what thou wilt shall be the whole of the law, and love as the law, love under will."

Satanic rituals abuse where a child is chosen to be a special one through whom the cultists will be able to receive power to receive power there must always be a sacrifice, the kingdom principle.

An infant or a child is chosen to be the living sacrifice unto satan. The child is subjected to numerous torturers and terrifying rituals where by demons are summoned to come into a child making him or her a literal storehouse or battery of satanic power that can be accessed by the cult members at will.

They use pentagrams that have special magic power and that is where most of our young gospel singers are being slaughtered, in the name of launching albums, they are taken to Serena, Hotel African and put in the middle of a pentagram and from that time that's where the inspiring songs stops.

Goats head sign represents satan. One time one of the cult pastors in the New Vision Newspaper was conducting a tour with the President at his farm, he was flashing the goats head sign with three middle fingers bent and leaving the thumb and little finger up, that's when the Israelites used to get a goat and pronounce all the sins of the people and send it in the wilderness, so satan says they got that goat back and that it represents satan as sin.

High Pop singer Shasha Fierce sang: "I have someone else that takes over when it's time for me to work and when I am on stage, this alter ego that I've created kind of protects me and who I really am."

The separating line between the church and the world has been all but obliterated, smoothed and deleted. Sins of the secular world, e.g. gays and divorce, are now approved by numbers of professing "Born Again"

Christians and copied as young people early in church. Religious leaders and pastors have adopted the techniques and styles of advertising like billboards, pausing with wives, boasting baiting or setting traps and exaggerating are carried on as normal procedure in church work. In Nambole they are detoothing people of God. Pastors demanding people to bring big money so that the Lord will bless them according to what they pledge and put in the coffers.

The moral climate is not that of the New Testament but of Hollywood and Broadway. Most evangelicals no longer Initiate - they Imitate and the world is the model. *12th February 2011*

CHAPTER THIRTY

NO MAN IS WORTHY TO SUCCEED UNTIL HE IS WILLING TO FAIL

PRAYER, "THE CLOUD OF UNKNOWING." God unto whom all hearts be open and unto whom no secret thing is hid, I beseech thee, so for to cleanse the intent of my heart with the unspeakable gift of Thy Grace, that I may perfectly love You and worthily praise You.

Prayer is effective and when it is not answered something is wrong. It becomes ineffective when Ye ask, and receive not, because ye ask amiss, that ye may consume it upon your lusts. James 4:3.

Furthermore, to pray effectively we must pray within the context of the World situation as God sees it, not by what the world thinks about itself, human rights activists should influence us, but also what God thinks about the World.

Prayer, O! God, let thy Glory be revealed once more to men though me if it pleases You, or without me or apart from me, it matters not. Restore thy church to the place of moral beauty that becomes her as the bride of Christ, through me or apart from me, only let this prayer be answered. O! God, honour whom thou will. Let me be used or overlooked or ignored. Amen.

No man is worthy to succeed until he is willing to fail. No man is worthy of success in spiritual activities until he is willing that the honour of succeeding should go to another, if God so wills e.g. John the Baptist.

God will allow His servant to succeed when He has learned that success does not make him dearer to God nor more valuable in the total scheme of things. Our great honour lies in being just what Jesus was and is. TO be accepted by those who accept Him, rejected by all who reject Him, loved by those who love Him and hated by everyone that hates Him. *13th February 2011*

CHAPTER THIRTY-ONE

HOPE, WHAT IS HOPE?

WHAT A TERRIBLE THING for man to get Old and have no hope, no gracious promise for the long eternity before him. Sis Alisa's Fellowship (Chicago).

Hope, what is Hope? Hope is like a promise, it is the ability to see a head positively even when you are surrounded with a negative concrete wall, Hope will make you hang on. Hope helps us to see differently where others see and feel doomed or hopeless. Hope tells us you can make it. You shall overcome, you shall reach there. Hope enables you to grow wings and fly where others are crawling. People perish when they lose hope.

We are living on hope and promise of our Lord, Do not let your hearts be troubled, John 14:1-3. In 1982 the Lord took me to heaven and around the Mansions He promised in John 14. From September 16th 1979 - 16th September 2001 I lived on hope when the Lord kept promising me that He was the only one who was going to return My son Peter who was kidnapped when he was 2 years and was returned after 22 years. It is hope which kept me going.

From 1971 – 1980s living in Uganda was like a nightmare,

only people who stood on the Word of God had Hope that God was going to deliver us from dictators with bloody regimes.

I worked in the office of Idi Amin from 1973 – 1979 but before the down fall of Iddi Amin the Lord showed me the end of his rule. saw him standing in the parking ground of the president's office as a statue of Nebuchadnezzar decorated with all his medals up to his knees. As I was watching he fell down on his face dead. The Lord said "Iddi Amin's rule is over get out of his office."

In 1996 I went to the village and found a young mother who had AIDS with 4 kids, her husband was dead and 2 of her kids and were given a few months to live, but when I went and introduced basket weaving, she started weaving baskets and I started paying her little money it brought her hope up and to now she is still living. *March 2011*

CHAPTER THIRTY-TWO

HOW TO OVERCOME FEAR

I WAS DISCUSSING with Sis Judi the power God has entrusted to man. Shared about Nikola Tesla, a Polish inventor who built tall towers and gathered energy in the outer space.

All night I was beading and fellowshipping with the Lord. In the morning in a dream, I saw as if I was in a class and each student was having a square field, this field was fitted with everything from the smallest to the biggest treasures.

This gave me a lesson that God has given each person the same measure of Spirit, created us in His Image, Gen. 1:27, He put Eternity in our hearts, yet man cannot find out the work which God has done from the beginning even to the end, Ecclesiastes 3:11.

Therefore, God has fitted in your square field everything, e.g. gold mines, oil fields, diamond mines, fresh water lakes, springs of Living Water, authority, power, etc.

It is in your ability to stir, activate yourself and find out who you are and what you can arrange and arrange to accomplish what was stored in you. In 1908 Nicholas Tessler, a man from Poland, when he found out the power he had before this great discovery of high technology he started building high towers and found out that if you go beyond the outer atmosphere you can gather energy which can cause catastrophes or vice versa. He stood in New York and directed this energy; he had gathered and threw it in Siberia, Russia in a forest of 1000 square miles. The energy consumed the trees in the forest and left it as tooth picks, without touching the ground to leave a crater. Up to now nothing grows in that area.

You have everything in your field depending on how you are going to use it.

16th March 2011

FEAR AND HOW TO OVERCOME IT, LADIES MEETING, Birmingham. Fear is the act of being afraid or scared of what is going on, about to happen or of the results of what has already taken place in past history.

Fear hinders one to see ahead, one only sees doom and helplessness. Fear tells you that you cannot make it, you will not reach there, you shall not overcome this, you shall not see your child. Fear will make you crawl instead of fly. Fear kills people before they mature to fulfill the purpose of the Lord. Fear drives away Hope, Faith, Patience and Long Suffering, e.g. 22 years waiting for Peter and 9 years for Robert.

Scriptures on Fear, about the Red Sea, Exodus 14:13; and Do not be afraid of sudden ... Proverbs 3:25.

Fear creates disease which is not there Dream, e.g. 11th February 2011: he makes people into believing his lies by throwing threats of disease in the bodies of people. It starts as pricking needle, one accepts it, he increases the pain instead of refusing it there and then; one goes to the doctor to inquire where they tell him or her she has breast cancer. In the end one is on taking drugs for a disease he or she has never had and the strong drugs start creating something else due to reaction.

How to overcome fear:

- confess the Word of God, Isaiah 55:10-11,
- speak it – declare it,
- believe it – do not doubt,
- walk it – Psalm 119:105,
- live it – Matt. 4:4, and
- have Faith in God.

When my mum passed away in January 1999, she left me 10 kids in the house, the youngest was 9 months. I trusted the Lord and left them in the house alone having faith that the Lord was going to keep them safe without me. *3rd April 2011*

CHAPTER THIRTY-THREE

I AM STANDING FOR MY NATION UGANDA

WE ARE LIVING in the Days of Daniel 12. I was flying from Birmingham Airport in Alabama to New Orleans Airport in Louisiana. I took the window seat and kept looking at the wing of Southwest aircraft as I was praying in the spirit. The Holy Spirit started talking to me in my spirit saying that man made these crafts which can fly in the air carrying hundreds of people from state to state, continent to continent. Man has not given God the glory but he considers himself a great engineer.

Manmade computers from big frames which used to fit in a big room, but now man has down sized it to fit in the palm of the hand. Man can now run and conduct business on remote and can do video conferencing wherever he is. Still he thinks he is generous in high tech and God is left out and not glorified.

Man has made ocean liners which can carry thousands of people, 8,000 excluding the crew, it carries cargo in a month it goes from US to African shores. The ocean liner builder is praised for the great wisdom, God who gives man wisdom is not mentioned anywhere. The Titanic ocean liner builders, before they launched it, boasted that "Even God Cannot Sink It" but after a few miles in the middle of the ocean it hit an iceberg and it sank. God proved them wrong.

Man has made shuttles to go to the moon 230,000 miles from the earth in a short space of time. But men considers that it is their great innovation. Nowhere is God given His right place as an initiator of all wisdom in man. These worldly people who do not put God first and give Him the glory in all what they have accomplished, there is no reward promised in all they have accomplished, it is all sinking sand.

YOU HAVE BEEN PROMISED A REWARD.

You have taken God at His Word; you are created in His Image, you have His Spirit, and He put eternity in your soul and promised you Eternal Life, You have a Reward promised. And the Teachers and those who are wise shall shine like the brightness of the firmament, and those who turn many to righteousness (to uprightness and right standing with God) shall give forth light like the stars forever and ever. Daniel 12:3, Matt. 13:43, (AMP).

But the people who know their God shall be strong and do great things, take action, shall stand firm and do exploits for God, Daniel 11:32. And they shall build the ancient ruins, they shall raise up the former desolations and renew the ruined city, the devastation of many generations. Isaiah 61:4.

Daniel 12, we are in the times of Daniel 12:4 and many will go back and forth. Now people are traveling back and forth, transit lounges are full of travelers. Knowledge and education shall be vastly increased, that's why you are seeing computer high-tech which has made the World and universe become like one global village.

Matthew 24 signs, Our Lord gave the answer of the end times when His disciples asked Him what will be signs and He told them e.g. famine - Ethiopia from 1970s to now,

Floods - New Orleans, 2004, earthquakes - Haiti and Chile February 2010, tsunami - Indonesia December 2006 and Japan March 2011, and wars - Iraq, Egypt, Tunisia, Yemen, Iran, Libya all in 2011.

Like the Master who was going away and gave talents to his Servants, Matt. 25:14-28, you were given a number of Talents, what have you done with them? On 16th March 2011 in the morning in a dream the Lord showed me as if we were in a classroom with other students, and each one was having a Square Field, in this field was fitted with everything from the smallest to the biggest. This means each one of us from the greatest person to the pauper God has given us the same measure of Spirit, it depends on you how you use your Square Field of treasure.

Therefore, child of God, Wake Up!!! and go in the fields to seek the Souls for the Lord, it's the only work which has a promised reward in Heaven. *5th April 2011*

ON 29TH FRIDAY THE WHOLE TOWN WAS ON FIRE WITH demonstrators of Walk to Work (Kiiza Besigye's factions). All offices were closed, I was with Clare and Emma at home. I had no sleep since I arrived. I called Pastor Nkata, Serwadda; Kyazze was outside on Seminar, Amos Kata said they were praying. SSV said the Lord is not looking for a group, He is looking for one to stand for the Nation.

I prayed "Lord it's me whom you have been waiting for. Here I am standing for my nation Uganda." At around 9.30pm I sent Emma to go and get me valium, when he brought them "a still small voice" advised me not to take it, even when I was about to swallow it. I had slept for a short time woke up in prayer.

I reminded the Lord about my Portion, I asked that for every soul which comes to the Lord through my Precedent Prayer for all Nations, all colours and all languages that in time of my Need may the Lord release this portion and my petition will be granted.

My Petions Prayer, Lord, may the prevailing situation in Kampala-Uganda be solved. No fires, no gun shots, no tear gas and no bloodshed. The Peace of the Lord returned in the whole of Uganda. 29th *April 2011*

Prayer, Interceding for the Nation. 30th *April 2011*

CHAPTER THIRTY-FOUR

PROSPERITY GOSPEL

AFTER RETURNING from the village my heart was so disturbed about the pastors and how they were behaving: Paul telling people that God cannot talk to anybody about him except the Lord talks to him only because he is the one who paid the price for a defense mechanism to stop whoever was to talk to deter him.

Pastor George Kahwa, an old pastor, advised Alan the young pastor that whenever a person comes to do a dedication, etc. should bring something; if not do not pray until he or she brings something; e.g. a young girl came and brought her child for dedication. Alan when holding the child in his arms asked the mother what have you brought to offer for the dedication, the mother said I have brought nothing. He refused to pray for the baby and said until when you will bring something and the girl never came back. What I learnt is the old pastor advising the young pastor into a doctrine of paying for God's Services which are freely given, If someone sins against a man, God will mediate for him, but if someone sins against the Lord, who can intercede for him, 1 Samuel 2:25.

Message, this morning the Lord spoke to my heart that: "Prosperity is not the indicator of righteousness, and righteousness is not indicated by prosperity." *6th May 2011*

CHAPTER THIRTY-FIVE

THE DEEP DARK FOREST

MESSAGE, You Are in the Deep Dark Forest, I got this message and shared it at Kyabaranga Church. That people are in a deep dark forest and they need to have a break through.

This world is like a deep dark forest and many people are lost in it. It is terrible to get lost in the forest with a dim breaking through light. Other people are tired and are about to give up because in the forest there are thickets with big trees which stands on the way obscuring you from seeing visions and forging ahead, e.g. religions, cults, and doctrines.

There are creeping plants which entangle you from walking fast, e.g. habits which creeps in and you ignore them until they entangle you; and fire plants that burns and you have to stop to scratch yourself, there are differ.ent hang-on plants which hangs on you, and a Columbus monkey trap plant that pulls you back and you have to stop to let it go, e.g. sins which you hang on saying only this!

There is wairimi, they build up in the trees when you disturb them, they will come down on you. Small flies which dances around your ears, e.g. Gossipers and rumours.

There are fallen trees so you cannot walk fast you have to stop to see how you are going to go about it jump it or go under, e.g. problems which lay across your way.

There are thorn plants and you cannot pass through them or touch them only to dodge them or cut them, i.e. people with sharp tongues.

In this deep dark forest there are snakes which will emit the terrible odor to scare you, and animals will be walking or growling to intimidate and to cause you to run, e.g. there are other denomination churches and people in authority with the noise they make to intimidate you.

If you have decided to walk out of this forest, you need determination and not listen the forest language of intimidation; close your ears, separate yourself and prepare to ignore the smell of snakes, the animals walking and growling, when they hear you coming and be determined they will run away.

In preparation get a sharp machete, a guard stick, a coat, a hat and boots, Therefore put on the full armour of God, so that when the day of evil comes, you may be bale to stand your ground, and after you have done everything to stand. Ephesians 6:13.

As you start clearing use your sharp machete to clear all objects which stands in your way, thorns and thorn trees, Columbus money trap plants, hang-on plants which sticks on you, (Sword). Your guard stick is very important, you lean on it for support, it swings overhead and with the machete both works together. The guard stick holds first a thicket and a machete cuts, parts and divides brush in portions to enable the machete to clear quickly, (Shield). A coat helps you to keep from the scratches of thorns and gives you warmth, (Breastplate). A hat protects from the stinging tiny wasps whose homes are high up in the trees as you cut down trees, their houses, they come down and pour on you, (Helmet of Salvation). A belt when you are cutting the forest you need to be firm, it supports your breath, and at times you get hungry it gives you sustenance, (Belt of truth). And boots are to protect your feet walking in the forest, as you walk you and break the thorns, (Shoes of Good News).

While in the deep dark forest walk and listen carefully because there are many residents living there who do not want you clear the forest, but the light will start shining there and expose them, they will discourage you, intimidate you, threaten you, harass you, attack you, etc. but you hang on and continue clearing your way.

After, when you have made your way you will start seeing the small dim light which will keep increasing until you have a break through into an opening and the sun will start shining. Few people, when they see the clearing, will be attracted to the light and want to walk in the light too. Even as the way has been cleared for them. Your life will become a light for someone else's pathway.

When you are still in the forest no one wants to join you or is interested to come and help because of fear, they will say no one has ever tried to cut that forest and He or she will not manage because it is hard saying let's see how far he will go and will discourage, intimidate, threaten you, and some will say nothing but just watch.

Many people like finished things because they are lazy, others want to see first how far you will go. Others who have ever been or are still in the forest will encourage you and stand with you. Yet others, when they cannot stop you, will come to see how far you have gone; when they see your determination to the point of a breakthrough, they will come to join you to finish up, due to the fact that they are starting to see light.

Therefore, you will be the light bearer, to tell people and teach people how to clear the forest, how to overcome the fears of the forest, you will advise them of the right armor to use and the attitude. 14th May 2011

*Nyamabuga Foundation Schools in 2018.
Our school has more than 400 students*

LEARN MORE AT WWW.NEEPUGANDA.ORG

ABOUT THE AUTHOR

The late Gertrude Kabatalemwa labored for the kingdom of God in her native land of Uganda. The burden of her heart was for the good news of Jesus to become deeply rooted, firmly grounded, and abundantly fruitful in the lives of the people of Uganda. In the past, she has served her nation as secretary to the president. She also functioned as Minister for the Development of Women.

At one point, she had taken in thirty-five of the orphans into her own village home, subsequently establishing Nyamabuga Foundational Schools for village children. Her plans include to prepare and equip these young people with the skills necessary to be able to lead their nation with a moral worldview.

Today, her children and those that she has poured into continue her work.

Through this book, you will be blessed by encountering the very large heart of this precious servant of God.

This is Gertrude's second book of the series "My Deepest Heart's Devotions."

facebook.com/neepuganda

www.ingramcontent.com/pod-product-compliance
Lightning Source LLC
Chambersburg PA
CBHW052135110526
44591CB00012B/1726